A BRIDGE ACROSS TIME

A
BRIDGE ACROSS
TIME

THE ROLE OF MYTHS IN HISTORY

James L. Henderson

*[Senior Lecturer in History and International Affairs
Institute of Education, London University]*

TURNSTONE BOOKS

Turnstone Books
37 Upper Addison Gardens
London W14

© copyright 1975 James L Henderson

First published in 1975

ISBN 0 85500 044 9

Type setting by Cold Composition Ltd
Tunbridge Wells, Kent.
Printed and bound in Great Britain by
The Anchor Press Ltd and William Brendon & Son Ltd
Tiptree, Essex

For M

Grateful acknowledgement is made to "The New Era" and to "Teaching History" for permission to make use of material in Chapter I and VI respectively, which previously appeared in their columns.

Contents

Foreword

There is a bridge across time, and we have to build it for ourselves. Its construction is a task partly of practical engineering and partly of creative imagination, and both of these are responses to the natural challenges of being alive. In this book I have tried to describe my own making of the bridge as an educationist and historian. It is based on forty years' experience of teaching in school and university, but it is informed by a lifelong attempt at learning how to make sense of personality — my own and other people's — and of the past both individual and collective.

Because the process of growing up is rooted in a sense of origins, that is where the two parts of the book start out from: the birth of the individual ego and the birth of civilisations are seen as analogous exercises in the extricating of the conscious from the unconscious; the transcendence of the individual life-span and the transcendence of historical eras are seen as analogous exercises in identifying and embracing the ultimate goal of existence, namely self-recognition by reality of itself. Personal identity is a transient phenomenon: the ultimately interesting question is how it can be transcended — Beethoven's Ninth Symphony and a Ming vase shake hands when Ludwig and all the Mings have vanished. In a poem called 'Epitaph'[1] R. S. Thomas seizes on just this point:

> The poem in the rock and
> The poem in the mind
> Are not one.
> It was in dying
> I tried to make them so.

And so do I!

Part one

EDUCATION

1

The Significance of the Past

"A man needs his strength as he lunges into the future, like a boxer in the ring; and the punch of it is not in his fist alone, but in the whole body of his past that makes him what he is."

(Freya Stark)[1]

There are layers of time in everything, including ourselves. 'Once upon a time' — that familiar phrase — can reveal them. When the emphasis is placed on the first of these four words, what stands out is the absolute uniqueness of each person and event: once, and once only, did the light fall just so in a Constable landscape; once, and once only, did Paul see a blinding light on the road to Damascus. About this aspect of each episode there hangs a kind of finality, but there is also its complement, where constancy is the keynote. However different the context of time and place and character, 'once upon a time' then promises security, reassurance and renewal. It seems to assert that behind all appearance of change there is a pattern of perpetuation, a quality of indestructibility, which witness to a time different from flying sequence.

As an old man introducing his autobiography, Carl Gustav Jung refers to this:

"Life has always seemed to me like a plant that lives on its rhizome. Its true life is invisible, hidden in the rhizome. The part that appears above ground lasts only a single summer. Then it withers away — an ephemeral apparition. When we think of the unending growth and decay of life and civilisations, we cannot escape the impression of an absolute nullity. Yet I never lost a sense of something that lives and endures

---

[1] et seq: For all sources of quotations, see Chapter Notes at back of book.

underneath the eternal flux. What we see is the blossom, which passes. The rhizome remains. In the end the only events in my life worth telling are those when the imperishable world irrupted into the transitory one."[2]

Such irruptions do occur and may be studied. They provide the evidence needed to convince us that human striving has a meaning, that it is not transitory and futile, that in fact nothing which has once really lived ever dies.

A common image of the past is of a time which stretches horizontally away behind the back of the present through thousands of years to some undiscovered and perhaps undiscoverable origin. Scattered along this time-track lie a number of more or less complex societies, of which Western civilisation is one. These have two features, the transience of all individual lives and most works and the durability of certain values. There appears to be a connection between the durability of those values and the degree of consciousness attained by the personalities and groups holding them. For instance, the obedience of Antigone in Sophocles' drama to "laws unwritten in the heavens" and the production of Anouilh's *Antigone* in wartime France in obedience to a law recognisably higher than the laws of the Germans, demonstrate that occupying forces are of the same order. Separated in chronological time by some two thousand years, they embody identical value judgements, namely that there exists a moral authority, transcending that of any temporary, temporal one, which has an absolute claim on all men capable of recognising it.

The quality of this consciousness pertains to that bridge across time, which it is the aim of this book to construct. Knowledge of it is best gained by professing a certain kind of faith and entertaining a particular intellectual hypothesis about the nature of man and the unconscious, one which in recent years has been increasingly explored by analytical psychologists. The latter will require elucidation; the former is tellingly evoked by the following reflection of the Irish thinker, 'A.E.', in correspondence with the late Helen Waddell:

"There is an Everlasting in which past, present and future are one, and when we brood on the past, it may be our intensity brings us to live in that brooded upon. It is not only in vision that we revisit the past: our hearts may sink into it and know what others have known."[3]

The nature of this time-transcending consciousness, as well as its far more frequent proneness to destruction by the passage of time, can be succinctly grasped by means of the following postulate. Suppose there are two sets of three individuals, whose lives are separated by a thousand years of chronological time, the first set for example living in Carolingian France and the second set in twentieth-century Britain. Two of these individuals in each set are time-bound, that is to say they have no existence or reality outside the narrow span of their own births or deaths and whatever legacy in children or works they may have bequeathed to their posterity. One in each set however has attained such a high degree of consciousness that each has more in common with his opposite number a thousand years of chronological time away than he does with either of his own contemporaries. This 'more' that they have could be constituted, for example, of the greater capacity for richness of emotional response or sharpness of intellectual acumen they possess as compared with the capacities of their respective contemporaries in chronological time. Whether they know that this is so, that is, discover that affinity of theirs, must depend on how far they have advanced on the bridge across time. The levels of consciousness of the other couple fall somewhere between these two previous extremes, so that they have intimations but not assurance of time-transcendence. This postulated phenomenon receives illumination from a remark by Herman Broch in his novel, *The Sleepwalkers*:

"Bertrand was struck by the fact that the world was full of people belonging to different centuries, who had to live together, and were even contemporaries; that accounted perhaps for their instability and their difficulty in understanding one another rationally; the extraordinary thing was that, nevertheless, there was a kind of human solidarity and an understanding that bridged the years."[4]

A consensus of Eastern and Western wisdom confirms this hypothesis, namely that after a certain height of consciousness has been attained, the limitations of material incarnation are transcended and may be known to be transcended. According both to Buddhist and Taoist doctrine it is possible during one lifetime or more so to cultivate the spiritual principle in oneself as to establish between it and the spirit of pure consciousness, the Atman and the Brahman, a bond which physical death does not dissolve. That, however, is only the case when the consciousness has been raised to a sufficiently high level.

To what, it may be asked, can be ascribed such varieties of heights and durabilities of consciousness? In suggesting an answer, it will be necessary to adopt another and equally indispensable view of the past, namely a vertical one. In an essay entitled 'Mind and the Earth' Jung supplies a helpful, though admittedly incomplete, analogy between the structure of human personality and an historic site:

". . . we have then to describe and to explain a building the upper storey of which was erected in the nineteenth century, the ground floor dates from the sixteenth century, and a careful examination of the masonry discloses the fact that it was reconstructed from a dwelling-tower of the eleventh century. In the cellar we discover Roman foundation walls, and under the cellar a filled-in cave, in the floor of which stone tools are found, and remnants of glacial fauna in the layers below. That would be a sort of picture of our own mental structures. We live in the upper storey, and are only dimly aware that our lower storey is somewhat old-fashioned. As to what lies beneath the superficial crust of the earth we remain quite unconscious . . .

"But the deeper we descend into the past the narrower the horizon becomes, and in the darkness we come upon the nearest and most intimate things, till finally we reach the naked rock floor, down to that early dawn of time when reindeer hunters fought for a bare and wretched existence against the elemental forms of wild nature. These men were still in the full possession of their animal instincts, without which their existence would have been impossible. The free sway of the instincts is not consistent with a powerful and comprehensive consciousness. The consciousness of primitives, as of the child, is of a spasmodic nature; his world, too, like the child's, is very limited. Our childhood even rehearses, according to the phylogenetic principle, reminiscences of the pre-history of the race and mankind in general. Phylogenetically as well as ontogenetically we have grown up out of the dark confines of the earth."[5]

Elsewhere Jung remarks:

"The psyche is not of today; its ancestry goes back many millions of years, individual consciousness is only the flower and the fruit of a season, sprung from the perennial rhizome beneath the earth; and it would find itself in better accord with the truth if it took the wisdom of the rhizome into its calculations."[6]

The premise we have just established about the structure of human personality compels us next to try to correlate the flight of time along the horizontal with the time taken by individuals and groups to grow vertically from unconsciousness towards consciousness; the attempt may lead us in the direction of that bridge across time for which we are seeking.

If poetic is more acceptable than psychological insight, reference could usefully be made to an observation of Rilke's to the effect that "our customary consciousness inhabits the apex of a pyramid, whose base in us (and in a sense beneath us) spreads to such breadth that, the further we find ourselves capable of letting ourselves down into it, the more generally do we appear to be included in the given facts, not dependent on time and space, of in the broadest sense worldly experience".

Rilke is convinced that "at some deeper cross-section of this pyramid of consciousness mere being could become an event for us, that inviolable presentness and simultaneity of all that which, in the upper 'normal' apex of self-consciousness it is granted to us to experience as mere sequence".[7]

Two principles of Jung's analytical psychology support the concept just sketched. First, there is the contention that the conscious derives from the unconscious, that the conscious part of human personality is supported and sustained by layers, first individual and then collective, of the unconscious. Above and below, light and dark are in a state of dynamic relationship and polarity to one another. The opposite of what is in the conscious is always found in the unconscious; for example, outwardly I smile upon my guest while inwardly I frown, or consciously I detest my rival while unconsciously I love him. This description of personality structure, somewhat mechanistically expressed but not so conceived, is simply posited by Jung as an essential part of his view of human nature. As to the origins of consciousness, he suggests two ways in which it seems to come about:

"The one is a moment of high emotional tension comparable to that scene in Wagner's Parsifal where in the instant of greatest temptation he suddenly realises the meaning of Amfortas's wound. The other is a contemplative condition, where representations move like dream images. Suddenly an association between two apparently disconnected and remote representations takes place, through which a great amount of latent energy may be released. Such a moment is a sort of revelation. In each case it is a concentration of energy, arising from an external or internal stimulus that brings about consciousness."[8]

To anticipate somewhat, we could say that history is the record of such concentrations of energy. Secondly, there is the Jungian concept of the collective unconscious as being constituted of archetypes or primordial images.

"The primordial image or archetype is a figure, whether it be a daemon, man or process, that repeats itself in the course of history whenever creative fantasy is freely manifested. Essentially, therefore, it is a mythological figure. If we subject these images to a closer investigation, we discover them to be the formulated resultants of countless typical experiences of our ancestors. . . . .

"The natural man is characterised by unmitigable instinctiveness. . . . The heritage that stands in opposition to this condition (i.e. consciousness) consists in the memory-deposits from all the experience of his ancestors. One is inclined to approach this assumption with scepticism because one thinks that 'inherited ideas' are meant. This is not the case. What is meant is rather inherited possibility of ideas, 'paths', that have been gradually developed through the cumulative experience of the ancestors. To deny the inheritance of the paths would be equivalent to denying the inheritance of the brain. To be logical such sceptics would have to maintain that the child is born with an ape's brain. Since, however, it is born with a human brain, this must grow or later begin to function in a human way, and apparently it will begin at the level of the most recent ancestors. Obviously this functioning remains deeply unconscious to the child. At first he is conscious only of the instincts, and all that opposes them is embodied in his visible parents. Thus the child has no idea that what stands in his way may be within himself. Rightly or wrongly, whatsoever interferes with him is projected upon the parents or surrogates. . . . Although our inheritance consists in physiological paths, still it was mental processes in our ancestors that created the paths. If these traces come to consciousness again in the individual experience and thus appear as individual acquisitions, they are none the less pre-existing traces which are merely filled out by the individual experience. Every impressive experience is such an impression in an ancient, but previously unconscious, stream-bed."[9]

The archetypes of the collective unconscious may therefore be thought of as continually manifesting themselves in symbolic and conceptual forms on the horizontal, sequential time-track of an individual's or a society's brief span of existence between birth and death. For example, the archetype of death and rebirth, the destiny of spirit's entry into nature's rhythms, takes symbolic form in the myth of Dionysus hundreds of years BC and also in the Stroller figure in Yeats's play, *The King of the Great Clock Tower*, in the twentieth century AD. It is a matter of time-bound expressions of timeless realities.

Such manifestation has the quality of a tension constituted of two opposing forces, an impulse towards conscious personality and individual responsibility and a contradictory impulse towards adherence or return to an unconscious state of irresponsibility. For example, anyone experiencing the challenge of growth must feel ambivalently towards the pain which inevitably accompanies the pleasure attending it: part of him feels the urge to accept and endure it, while another part feels 'I can't bear it' and yearns to return to mother's apron string. The product of such conflict may be called the diagonals of consciousness, and these are the struts of which is constructed that bridge across time on which we may take our stand if we sufficiently care to do so. If we do not so care, or if external circumstances are so adverse that they actually prevent us from so caring, then all of our transitory ego identity, the corpse that is buried or burnt, simply drops back into the anonymous source from which it derived and possesses no ultimate, historical significance whatsoever. It is in fact all that part of us, which has not transcended the secondary characteristic of individual ego-existence by trans-mutation into spirit-self, independent of time and space. It is what has failed to make the passage from original 'uncon-scious anonymity' to eventual 'conscious anonymity'.[10] It is all that of Brahman which has not yet got to know itself in Atman. Because it is only a few at any time who have thus disciplined themselves and thus been blessed, there are far more of us to die and suffer corruption, and far fewer to survive. That must be the meaning of one of the few 'big dreams' I have been vouchsafed. As I awoke from sleep I heard a voice saying to me quite unsensationally and quietly but also quite incontrovertibly: "You can't be bothered to learn how not to die." Because most of us do not bother, most of us do not achieve immortality.

The development of the idea of death as a problem occurs only with the increasing growth of ego-consciousness: for it is when the ego becomes aware of itself as a prisoner of that horizontal, linear time, which unrolls from past to future, that the historical consciousness has either to learn how to transcend time by scaling the diagonal struts or admit its meaninglessness. That such an effort of transcendence can be made successfully is well demonstrated by R. C. Johnson, who has shown most skilfully how the disciplines of natural science, psychical research and religion can contribute to the accomplishing of that task.[11]

Before proceeding further, it will be useful to summarise the argument thus far. There is a need, it has been suggested, for two views of the past, a horizontal and a vertical one, that of historical sequence, the other, that of personality growth. These views are countenanced by much traditional wisdom teaching, particularly of the East, by the records of aesthetic experience and by the findings of analytical psychology. The last named provided us with two principles, the derivation of the conscious from the unconscious and the function of archetypes; their combination indicated a perpetual state of conflict between the pull of consciousness and the pull of unconsciousness which in historical terms could be called the pull of the future and the pull of the past — the resultant lines of tension being named the diagonals of consciousness. These struts express their interrelationship and support our bridge across time.

The past needs to be thought of as in us now, as part of our unconscious personality structure and also as behind us chronologically in consciousness. Progoff has well indicated the nature of this concept in the following passage:

"The psyche has depth downward, but it also extends backwards, across, through time, so that somehow history is latently contained and unconsciously expressed in each individual. This is Jung's great thesis for the study of history in terms of the psyche. It makes possible a dimension of time-study in which time is a unitary category for personality and social history."[12]

All of man that is making for conscious personality must regard the characteristics of the unconscious as belonging to an earlier, more primitive, archaic state, but also as his very source of life, his roots, his past. An example of the process would be a quite primitive upthrust of lust or greed, originally just instinctual forces but now regarded with disfavour or at least wariness by consciousness. The point is that Tarquin's rape of Lucrece in the past and a contemporary's largely unconscious desire to rape his pin-up girl form part of the same 'unitary category', and understanding of the motivation of the former can help to control the latter.

In case such a concept of the nature and function of history should appear startling, it may help to recall here a Hindu sanction for it. The Indian world picture is constituted out of two kinds of time: one is 'curved time', exemplified in cyclical terms of existence emanating from and leading to a timeless state of godhead; in our terminology this would correspond to the horizontal time-track. The other Indian time is that of individual man engaged in working out his

Karma, a kind of zigzag time reflecting his good and evil features, and this would correspond to what in our terminology we have called personality. The link between the two is provided by the diagonal of consciousness. It is tempting to think that it was some such link which the Russian philosopher Berdyaev was seeking to establish when he wrote the following sentence: "Thus the real goal of the philosophy of history is to establish a bond between men and history, between man's destiny and the metaphysics of history."[13]

Our image of history, time past, is therefore that of a record of the growth of human consciousness on the diagonal struts created by the tension between the pull of the past and the unconscious and the pull of the future and the conscious. Our study of history becomes significant, so satisfying the demands of what Whitehead called the 'insistent present', only in so far as we recognise and experience the reality of these diagonals. In other words there has to be a capacity for diagonals in ourselves to respond to the diagonals of others.

The 'dimension of time-study' to which Progoff refers is one in which the essence of the human predicament — the dilemma implicit in being alive at all — never changes, however much the expression of it may vary. It is the archetypes which determine the kind of experience we have, but it is we as individuals who determine what we actually experience. Within its 'unitary category' there are infinite numbers and varieties of manifestations of a certain number of archetypes. When these occur at a high level of consciousness we can, if ourselves sufficiently well-endowed, respond to them wherever they happen to be placed chronologically. Recognising and naming a Beethoven sonata, a Socratic dialogue, a Newtonian insight, we call what they represent civilisation and are sustained by its perennial truth. When they occur and persist, as is much more often the case, at a low level of consciousness, then too we respond — often very strongly — from our own low levels, but we hardly ever know them or admit them in ourselves, and when we detect them in others we call them barbarism.

I hope that I have expressed with sufficient clarity the image of a relationship between the flight of time and the growth of consciousness. What needs to be held in the mind is the culmination of this relationship in an awareness of real identification with a transcendental and timeless reality, independent of what mortals call death.

> Never the spirit was born, the spirit shall cease to
>   be never.
> Never was time when it was not, end and beginning are
>   dreams.
> Birthless and deathless and changeless, the spirit endureth
>   for ever,
> Death does not change it at all, dead though the house of
>   it seems.
>
> (Gita)

A full and confident knowledge of this truth is what we exist for: failure in this undertaking can lead only to despair, a plight which two very different writers discerned as the desperate one of post-Christian Western culture catastrophically threatened by the 'death of its house'.

In a poem called 'Vastness' Tennyson wrote:

> What is it all, if we all of us end in being
>   Our own corpse-coffin at last,
> Swallowed in vastness, lost in silence, drown'd
>   In the depths of a meaningless past?
> What but a murmer of gnats in the gloom, or a
>   Moment's answer of bees in their hive?

In an essay entitled 'Rilke and the Concept of Death' William Rose put his finger exactly on the value of that German poet's contribution:

"If death is to be regarded as the final blossoming of life, something to which we are working up and not a running-down of the machine, it must logically be something more than mere annihilation. . . . Rilke is absorbed in the problem of death because he regards it as fulfilment of life."[14]

A passage from one of Rilke's letters brings the whole challenge to an eloquent climax.

". . . how is it possible to live when the fundamentals of this our life are so completely incomprehensible? When we are always inadequate in love, wavering in our determination and impotent in the face of death? In this book, written under the profoundest inner compulsion, I have not managed to conquer my amazement over the fact that for thousands of years humanity has been concerning itself with life and death (not to speak of God) and yet, even today (and for how much longer?) stands in front of these primary, these immediate tasks (strictly speaking the only ones we have — for what else have we to do?) so helplessly, so pitiably, caught between terror and evasion like the veriest beginners. Is it not incredible? My own amazement over this fact whenever I give way to it drives me into the greatest confusion and then into a sort of horror; but behind the horror there is something else, something so immediate and yet transcending all immediacy, something so intense that I cannot decide with my feelings whether it be like fire or ice. . . .

"And so, you see, the same thing happened with Death. Experienced and yet not to be apprehended by us in his reality, always overshadowing yet never quite acknowledged by us, violating and surpassing the meaning of life from the very beginning, he too was banished and excommunicated so that he should not continually interrupt us in our search for this meaning. . . . More and more the suspicion grew up against him that he was the anti-thesis, the opponent, the invisible opposite in the air; the end of all our joys, the perilous glass of our happiness from which we may be spilled at any moment. . . . Nature, however, knew nothing of this banishment which we have somehow managed to accomplish — when a tree blossoms death blooms in it as well as life. . . . And love too, which bedevils our arithmetic so as to introduce a game of Near and Far . . . love too has no regard for our divisions but sweeps us, trembling as we are, into an infinite consciousness of the whole. Lovers do not live from fear of the Actual . . . of them one can say that God is nourishing them and that death does not harm them: for they are full of death because they are full of life."[15]

Any move out of this impasse involves an appeal to the actuality of that part of human personality which, unlike the physical body and the conscious ego, is in fact deathless. In his book *Cosmos and History, the Myth of the Eternal Return*[16] Eliade has pointed the way:

"The death of the individual and the death of humanity are alike necessary for their regeneration. Any form whatever, by the mere fact that it exists as such and endures, necessarily loses vigour and becomes worn; to recover vigour it must be re-absorbed into the formless if only for an instant; it must be restored to the primordial unity from which it issued; in other words, it must return to 'chaos' (on the cosmic plane), to 'orgy' (on the social plane), to darkness (for seed), to water (baptism on the human plane). . . ."

The two most dramatic attempts to break this circle and form history into a kind of linear progressivism have been the pseudo-Messianism of an incomplete Christianity and Marxism, neither of which, however, has been able to save man from what Eliade calls the 'terror of history', his finding himself literally at a dead end.

Not so to conceive of death requires of most of us moderns in Western civilisation a tremendous effort to think differently. For, with the decay of genuinely held convictions on Christian lines about human survival, the assumption has crept in that, so far as we personally are concerned, when we die that is the end of everything. Instead of this happening we can learn to adopt a different attitude to death by coming to view it as that part of the historical process, described here already as the disappearance back into 'unconscious anonymity' of all the secondary characteristics of human individuality. Accordingly nothing dies that has attained a certain level of consciousness, and it is towards the attainment of such a level that the 'whole creation travaileth and groaneth'.

2

The Theme of Origin in Education

'Within, though: who could avert, divert, the floods of origin flowing within him?'

(Rilke)[1]

The question of the origin of life inevitably crops up in all learning about human experience, nowhere more so than in the subject of history. 'Once upon a time', 'in the beginning': these are unavoidable utterances, which must occur before 'what happened next and what is happening now.' How far do and how far can all of us alive today share the same image of and conviction about our origins? I am going to try to suggest the measure in which we can and the reason why we should.

There are two equally valid, different but complementary approaches to this problem, one mythical, the other scientific, each inadequate on its own but extremely hard to relate to one another in a significant unity. Yet this must be the aim of any teacher trying to help his pupils of the second half of the twentieth century make common sense of their ancestry.

"For surely it is folly to preach to children who will be riding rockets to the moon a morality and cosmology based on concepts of the Good Society and of man's place in nature that were coined before the harnessing of the horse?"[2]

Our own Western myth of origin, itself a product of the East, is the story of Adam and Eve in the Garden of Eden: it requires no re-telling here. Rather, let us set it side by side with an Indian one:

"In the beginning this world was soul (Atman) alone in the form of a person. Looking around, he saw nothing else than himself. He said first: 'I am' . . . He was, indeed, as large as a woman and a man closely embraced. He caused that self to fall (pat) into two pieces. Therefrom arose a husband (pati) and a wife (patni)."

These two myths together with many others from all over the earth's surface seem to contain the same fundamental meaning, namely that originally there was a cosmos, unaware of its own nature, and that this cosmos then started — how and why is always just accepted as a mystery — to become self-conscious. This process was attended by the loss of unity and the appearance of duality in the form of opposites generally and the two world parents, male and female, in particular. Behind every child's individual parent figures there are ranged these archetypal ones, rooted in an unfathomable mystery, which is yet recognised as pregnant with a potential design and from which there has always emanated and still emanates a sense of authority.

The following extract from an article in the *Times* could be taken as a specimen passage for the scientific assessment.

Recent Speculations on the Origin of Life

Ideas in Plenty, but no Answers yet

From our Science Correspondent

Science and Medicine Today

Speculations on the origin of life are interminable; they could be ended only by its creation in conditions bearing some relation to those thought to have been probable in past ages on the earth. They are also recurrent — because from time to time new facts are discovered, or new ideas originated, which bear in some way on the problem.

There has been a recent discussion in the United States. It was held by the American Association for the Advancement of Science; and, again, some new facts were available. The most important were about the extent to which simple raw materials could be built up by heat alone into substances significant for living organisms. Compared with, say, the beginning of the present century, none of the three most important changes in the situation are, in fact, very recent.

One of them has been a growing acceptance, stimulated by increasing knowledge of viruses, that there seems to be no clear-cut distinctions between what is living and what is not. Degree of organisation is obviously important. So, too, is the ability to maintain, by dynamic change, a roughly static advantage in energy above surroundings; like a celluloid ball, as it has been said, supported by a water jet. And so, again, is ability to reproduce.

No one of these properties is exclusive to life. For each of them it is a help that there should be a boundary — the cell membrane — between what is organised and its surroundings. In practical terms, the acquisition of such a boundary must have been a critical step. But to say that "what is living is living cells" fails to satisfy even the minimum requirements of definition. And the absence of clear-cut distinctions is left as one point that has emerged.

The other two main points can be stated shortly. One of them is that, the further biochemistry advances, the more complicated does the organisation of a living cell appear. The gap between a random mixture of chemicals and a functioning cell is thus more striking. But it is a gap in complexity and arrangement — not in principle.

Striking Gap

The other main point is a reflection of progress in astronomy. Many more planets — of other stars, even in other galaxies — must be supposed to have had histories comparable with that of the earth. The scope for the invoking of unusual or improbable conditions — should that be necessary — is thus greater.

The stage on the earth can be set more closely. The atmosphere surrounding its still molten crust is likely to have consisted largely of hydrogen and its similar compounds — methane, ammonia, hydrogen sulphide and water vapour. From this atmosphere, hydrogen would have been lost from the top; into it, from the slowly crystallising crust, there would have been forced quantities of water and carbon dioxide. But in ammonia, carbon dioxide, and water, we have already the raw materials of a chemistry which could become life. With further cooling, rains would have fallen and oceans been formed; they would have been uneasy cauldrons at first.

For building up to proceed, sources of energy would be needed. One possibility is high-energy ultra-violet radiation from the sun. How much of it would have penetrated to sea level depends on further assumptions. There would in any case have been violent vertical movements in the atmosphere, so that material formed high in it would have been carried rapidly to lower levels. For the same reason, thunderstorms would have been frequent, and effects from lightning discharge could be invoked. A third source of energy was the heat of the oceans.

After describing some of the most recent ideas about the source of energy the article concludes: "There are thus ideas in plenty — and will, no doubt be more. But the putting forward of a new idea, even of new evidence, does not mean that answers are yet in sight."

So it would appear that the scientific account has a great deal to offer about the conditions which seem to be essential for what we call life to appear, but nothing at all definite about that which causes the conditions to occur in the first place. On this subject there can only be conjecture, assumption and assertion, amounting, however, to a lowest common multiple of a hypothesis. This is to the effect that man can properly regard himself as the most articulate product of a process with an unknown origin, a process with at any rate marked characteristics of a teleological kind, that is to say not in Sir Arthur Eddington's words 'a mere fortuitous concourse of atoms'. Furthermore he is able to share in the means whereby this process occurs more and more consciously, but in order to do so he needs to remain constantly aware of his roots. This is what differentiates him from the animals, for man "no longer knows, but knows that he knows. . . . Man discovers that he is nothing else than evolution become conscious of itself."[3] This kind of hypothesis should at long last bridge the gap between science and religion, for it should prove acceptable to both those who admit the reality of the process but do not desire or feel able to postulate a God as directing it, and those who require for their spiritual contentment a theological sanction: both admit of an evolutionary purpose at work commanding his respect and capable of being affected by man himself.

Sir Julian Huxley has summarised admirably the global significance of such a concept, namely that of the 'unification of human awareness':

"Some general view of human destiny is surely the indispensable educational basis for an unfragmented culture. Yet this task is now largely relegated to the sidelines, often under the head of religious teaching. It could, however, become the unifying core of our educational theory and practice, because at last the increase of our knowledge is providing such a view, both comprehensive and relevant to the present state of the world. The unifying concept is evolution."[4]

Contemporary man can now be taught to peer down into his past and to discern how human consciousness grew out of a conflict between instinct and spirit, archetype and idea, collective agglomeration and distinctive individuation. He can observe how it was that experience of that conflict historically, which he can verify on the pulses of his own personality in the present, led his ancestors to formulate laws of living. How quickly or how slowly these laws became established depended on types of environment, distribution of intelligence and a host of other complicating factors. Modern man has then to learn how the rudiments as well as the refinements of socio-political consciousness developed through a tension between a society's archetypal and conceptual relationships to its origins, to its neighbours and to its ultimates.

Man's earliest experience of his origins must have been an ambivalent one: love of all the things which plainly nourished him and hate of those elements of his natural environment which so often menaced and shattered his security. For example there was the river which blessedly irrigated his land but could also rise and flood out his homestead. Linked to this kind of ambivalence was a parallel one, common to all sons and daughters, namely the feelings of love and hate towards their parents. For example, there is the caring parent whose attitude to the child is one of unconditional love, which, however, necessarily appears now in positive now in negative form. You are the mum I like because you feed me: you are the mum I dislike because this very love of yours applies the laws of digestion to me and prohibits me from making a pig of myself.[5] As primitive man began to discriminate between his own previously instinctive absorption in and identification with this twin matrix and a feeble brave something in him − the prototype of consciousness − battling against it, the rudiments of social consciousness and elementary group living were born. A discriminatory faculty in the management of his social relationships was the outcome of these creative contradictions between two forces experienced by early man. It was the power derived from this nascent consciousness of dual origin which enabled him to strike roots however tenuous, to entrench himself and his nearest in some kind of encampment against the hitherto irresistible natural driving forces that just blew him into and along an unexamined existence. He had learnt the beginning of that respect for nature's authority, combined with his own skills in wooing her, which were eventually to blossom in civilisations.

From a universal mythology of origin to the formulation of it in religious terms, mankind struck balances over the ages between archetype and idea. As he evolved a more or less rational explanation of where he had come from, this gave him the necessary solidarity of shared conviction to provide the needed sanctions for common modes of living. Coming from somewhere, he believed he belonged somewhere, that he had indeed an earthly habitation: he was learning to live with his guilt about the past because of his inevitable repudiation of it and also with his pride in it because of what it had enabled him to become.

From nomadic tribe to settled village community, from city state and civilisation to the early empires of the ancient world, these units increased in the size of their social consciousness as derived from a shared consciousness of human origin. It is precisely this shared consciousness of origin that we today have to recapture but on a global, not a partial, scale. A condition of so doing is to recognise, admire and transmit to our children that sense of reverence for the past which I have already discussed.

This means that careful attention must be paid to the childhood years of future world citizens: their infant experiences need to be contrived by the elders responsible for them in terms of psychological, developmental laws and of such environmental factors as climate, culture patterns and a material standard of living, these being now no longer separate but indivisible.

It can be assumed then that children everywhere have their images of reality determined at an early age by a combination of the influences of the archetypal, primordial image of origin, general and parental, and of particular homes and social structures in which they are born. Where the latter are of a homogeneous nature they tend to correlate with relative harmony to the archetypal pattern. Where this is not the case, as for example in our contemporary Western society, the correlation is largely ineffective, and so children in that situation are exposed to a particularly difficult task of personality and group integration.

Joseph Campbell has expressed this dilemma very well in the following passage, which makes an excellent text for the exposition of how we have to move from a non-homogeneous world society in embryo to a homogeneous one in actuality:

". . . it has been the general custom in traditionally based societies to reorganise the common human inheritance of infantile imprints in such a way as to conduct the energies of the psyche from the primary system of reference of infantile dependency into the sphere of the chief concerns of the local group . . . one is linked to one's adult role by being identified with a myth. . . . Pleasure, power and duty: these are the systems of reference of all experience on the natural level of the primitive societies."[6]

Accepting the hypothesis of 'the common human inheritance of infantile imprints', we must next surely ask, what are the various primary systems of reference in our own and other people's societies? Answers to this question will reveal a wide difference in, for example, the way in which babies are fed, the dominance of matriarchal or patriarchal presences, the degree of aggressiveness or cooperation displayed in the relationship between the elders and their young in any group. These too will to varying extents be influenced by the style of life of a particular adult society, rural or urban, for example. Yet, however diverse the methods by which the 'energies of the psyche' are conducted, all societies have such devices, and the gist of my argument is that in the present state of the world they need to be, not identical, but sufficiently similar, to be capable of producing common behaviour in those who have been exposed to them. In other words there has to be a deliberate modification of variety, if the span of the local group (including the nation state) is to be widened sufficiently to support a world that is one.

Because man 'is linked to his adult role by being identified with a myth', we next have to ascertain what is a viable myth today for the necessary linking. It is possible to give a preliminary kind of answer in terms of the three 'primary systems of reference', remembering that these were almost exclusively acted upon in primitive societies unconsciously, but that they now need to be sufficiently integrated into consciousness to become operative and unifying on a world scale. Pleasure, power and duty are three bonds by means of which every human being is riveted to his origin, both collective and individual. If, therefore, a similar global approach to these primary systems of reference can be established in early infancy everywhere, the foundation for a world society will have been firmly laid.

First there is the law of weaning, namely that every stage of differentiation involves a mixture of pleasure and pain to be accepted and endured, a blend of love for the source of nourishment which makes this advance possible and of hate for it because of the dependence on it which it implies. Unless sufficient allowance is made for the expression of the negative as well as the positive emotion, true growth will be stunted and twisted: "the outraged in infancy (whether by too much love or too much hate) are the criminals of maturity".[7] Unless prejudice is permitted its legitimate roots in childhood, it will produce illegitimate (that is, socially poisonous) fruit in adulthood. Therefore the myth or belief for general acceptance is to the effect that the pleasure-pain of weaning is something to be welcomed not rejected, that there is purpose in Amfortas' wound.

Secondly there is the law which demands of every child that in time he learns how to deal with those natural feelings of inferiority inevitably engendered by his smallness of body and personality in comparison with the grown-ups looming up over him. If his parents and teachers do not enable him to do so by judiciously provided occasions for the expression of his enjoyment of power over himself and others, he will inevitably develop an 'inferiority complex' with its attendant symptoms of aggressiveness and bellicosity. So here the myth or belief for general acceptance is that man needs to exercise his power instinct, and channels for it must be provided, excluding now the universally suicidal one of war.

Thirdly there is the law of authority, namely that every growing human organism requires some kind of external authority, which he can gladly obey if he is to learn eventually how, voluntarily to obey himself. For, as Herbart remarked, "the moral man commands himself". However timeless and authentic the parental archetype is, the symbol of 'God the Father' is no longer universally available or valid. Yet, as Dostoievsky wrote, "The man who bows down to nothing can never bear the burden of himself." What can the people of our world bow down to? All we can say here is that the myth or common belief for general acceptance is that there does exist in the cosmos something to which we all owe a duty. Perhaps Albert Schweitzer's phrase, 'reverence for life', best describes this spiritual stance. Practice in fulfilment of it can best take place through experience of obeying the laws of home. As I shall try to demonstrate, it should be possible to devise a curriculum by means of which all children everywhere receive the same basic education regarding the laws of their homes, that is, their home in time and space as well as their own individual homes. The particulars of this instruction will be infinitely various but they will be presented as stemming from a common origin and pursuing a common purpose.

Because, to paraphrase Collingwood,[8] man learns what he

can do from what he has done, the earliest lullabies, nursery rhymes and fairy stories, told by mother to young child, have a vital and definitive function. They are the medium by means of which the infant is gradually weaned to accept the destiny of his humanity, of learning what he can do from what others in his name before him have done. They are the channel through which his mother and other grown-ups of the family help him to draw nourishment from the original, mysterious bestower of life, whose discipline they respect together. It is vitally necessary to discern the two aspects of early childhood educational experience in the past, its manifest content and its latent significance. Several examples now follow, all of which are meant to demonstrate the theoretical contention that all true learning occurs on the diagonal of consciousness created by the tension between vertical and horizontal, psychological and historical, personal and collective apprehensions of the past. The learning takes place as and when the young child's and primitive man's creative fantasy is engaged and his level of consciousness thereby raised (see Chapter I).

In all three of the examples below there will be found in however naive a manner the enactment of a ritual drama, which possesses both archetypal and individual resonances. First there are nursery rhymes:

> Dance, little baby, dance up high:
> Never mind, baby, mother is by;
> Crow and caper, caper and crow,
> There, little baby, there you go;
> Up to the ceiling, down to the ground,
> Backwards and forwards, round and round:
> Dance, little baby, and mother shall sing,
> With the merry gay coral ding, ding a ding ding.

The manifest content of these lines is clear and simple, evoking by the rhythm of its words the primal play scene between mother and child: the keynote of the verse, adventurous playing within secure limits, up and away from the past, crowing and capering, but "mother is by". The latent significance of it is easily discerned in the baby's behaviour, the response of his body, the delighted smile on his face, the sudden wail of fear if the throw is too high or the maternal arms unsteady. The significant point is that the nursery rhyme, properly offered to the child, makes a whole appeal to him wholly — it absorbs him consciously and unconsciously, he learns in the experience by means of the association of archetype with ideas.

A second example is:

> Little Miss Muffet
> Sat on a tuffet,
> Eating her curds and whey.
> There came a big spider
> And sat down beside her
> And frightened Miss Muffet away.

Once again a straightforward enough tale at the level of manifest content, the picture of any little girl eating her dinner and being frightened by the approach of a fearsome-looking animal. It is in the latent significance of the lines that we must look for the clue to their perennial fascination, and at once the archetypal motif is discernible — beauty and the beast, innocence and experience, good and evil — the spider traditionally symbolic of the devouring maw of the primeval mother, of the ever-present threat to consciousness from the unconscious. The child who has taken delight in this nursery rhyme has had a twofold learning experience. Manifestly he has been introduced by means of a word picture to the reality of living, namely that beauty and the beast live next door to one another; latently the symbolism and rhythmic presentation of the story have stirred ancestral memories in him and so helped him both to break and to keep connection with the past.

A third example is:

> Jack Sprat could eat no fat,
> His wife could eat no lean;
> And so between them both you see,
> They licked the platter clean.

Here is an ordinary enough scene, immediately recognisable in terms of his own conscious knowing by every child in the earliest days of his feeding experience. Beneath the surface of manifest content, however, there is quite plainly a wealth of latent significance, consisting of the racial wisdom that knows of and respects the law of the opposites — Blake's 'no progressions without contraries'. Once again the child who delights in the rhyme is feeding upon the past with his conscious intellect and at the same time with his unconscious psyche, and therefore he is learning from it.

Next let us take a specimen fairy story:

"Once upon a time there lived a noble prince, whose palace lay at the foot of a mountain. One day he heard to his dismay that the beautiful lady whom he loved and hoped to marry had been captured by a terrible giant, who lived in a cave on the mountain side. He set forth to rescue her and met a lion, who said to him: 'Oh Prince, I will help you to overcome the giant and rescue your fair lady on one condition, that when this is done, you will kill me.' Hardly believing him the Prince agreed, and together they succeeded in killing the giant and rescuing the lady. Then he had to keep his part of the bargain. So he stabbed the lion to the heart, and from his dead body there sprang a lovely boy who, it turned out, had been cast into animal's form by a wicked enchanter but who was now set free, and the Prince and Princess lived happily ever after."

The manifest content of this tale is familiar enough, and its main features can be found anywhere in the world's literature, but what gives it its latent significance is the archetypal quality of its situation and characters. The Prince, Princess, giant and lion, the beautiful boy, as well as the palace, the cave and the mountain are all archetypes of person and place and so strike deeply into the whole being of the listening child who himself is of them and needs exercise with all of them if he is to grow eventually into a whole personality. It is worth noting that this kind of story appears to be particularly suitable for the age phase of about three to five, when psychologically the young child would appear to be having his first main round of encounter with his parents, when he is beginning to be able and to dare to say "I" rather than to refer to himself in the third person, a truly heroic task in the face of the giant parent figures, for which he needs the help of all the helpful animals he can find and enlist on his side.

The role of the story-teller is important because it is by his manner and character that a protective relationship between him and the child can and must develop. This will enable the immature organism to endure the tension of the tale, especially with regard to its negative, destructive side — the ferocious look and roar of the lion and the terror of the giant. Any attempt to exclude the negative is misguided sentimentality; for it is the absolutely essential opposite to the positive, without which no flash of communication can occur. Yet it must not be too negative, just as in the weaning process there can be no sudden jump from milk to roast beef. Moreover, the child himself very often has a kind of innocent wisdom, which warns the adult where to draw the line. Very often when the tale approaches some incident which is too awful for the child to bear, he will quickly slip off the adult's knee, close the book or simply say, "I don't want any more," and then he must be respected absolutely.

It is worth pausing to reflect on the elements of evil and sacrifice as they enter into these early stories, because through them the child is being introduced to the deepest experience of human existence, namely the fact of death and renewal. A modern poet has successfully married archetypal wisdom with sophisticated understanding in the following verses,[9] which could well serve as a paradigm for teachers:

THE NEED FOR DYING

And the wolf said, 'You must kill me'. — Fairy Story

They could not have outstripped the witch's daughter,
Got up unpoisoned from the ogre's feast,
Or fished the Queen's lost ring out of the water,
Without this suppliant and gentle beast,
Who since they gave it bread and pulled the thorn out,
Lent all its secret wisdom to their quest,
Forgave them each misdeed, until one morning,
Beyond their foul enchantment they were blest.
But then it turns towards the ransomed lady
And sea-changed princeling, whom no spells could part,
And murmurs earnestly, 'And now the promise,
Take your bright sword and plunge it in my heart.'

Of course they shrink away and offer riches
Broad water-meadows and a golden stall,
But at the last yield to the beast's imploring
And deal the fatal stroke that severs all.

Out of its blood, then, and the rags and tatters
Of fur and membrane on the stubble corn,
All glistening on his new, most lucky morning,
A second time the King's lost son is born.
He needed such a death stroke to redeem him
Of reptile, animal, or bird of prey;
And yet without this creature and its knowledge
How could the spell-bound children find their way
Through all those convolutions of the forest?
His night it was that guided them each day.

I mean that always on our star-crossed journey
That which we are is helpless to decide
Between the sheeptrack and the posted highway,
Until we drop the reins and cease to guide
Our pacing animals who smell direction
Blown softly through the gap where our will died.
No whip or spur of furious intention
But checks their speed unravelling the dark,
And if the Master bellows out his orders,
Before the abyss, then, no hound will bark.

I think he is the night, this lost companion,
And that in dreams and blood he lends us speech,
And seeing, with no eyes, that catch a meaning
Our organs of the day could never reach;
If humble as the lovers of the story
We bend down low to his insistent breath,
And turn a deaf ear to the witch's calling.
But why must we reward him by his death.

The faithful guide who led us through confusion?
Well, all the rituals say that he must die,
This Eros of the night, and his blind wisdom
Be changed within the twinkling of an eye.
I do not think his bull, white wolf, or stallion
Have any knowledge of their future Lord.

They only know that when their task is finished
They seek the desolation of the sword.
Perhaps, one day, we'll leave the witch's kingdom,
And thrust our childhood foliage apart;
Oh, may we then be altar, priest and victim,
A sharp, bright clarity, and pierce the heart.

The very first verse of the poem enunciates the truth that
life's tasks, however lofty, cannot be accomplished without
the aid of the instincts, however lowly. Yet 'beyond the foul
enchantment' we cannot be blessed except at a price, namely
the sacrifice of that which we hold dearest in the whole
world: an utterly paradoxical thing to have to do! By this
means, however, 'the king's lost son is born', redeemed by
and through his instinctive nature. In verse four the poet
offers a more specific interpretation of the myth, which
could be summarised as "trust your instincts". It is the night
of the dark unconscious, says verse five, which will teach us
wisely if only we will suffer it to and yet not succumb to it.
But why is all this painful sacrifice necessary, muses the poet
in his final verse, and the only answer to which he can gesture
without defining it, is that it is the price of self-knowledge,
for the sake of which we exist as men and women. The adult
teacher or parent must at any rate have begun to leave the
witch's kingdom, if the children he is caring for will, after
many years, "thrust their childhood foliage apart".

This in turn means that the story-teller must possess or
cultivate the knack of moving his narrative to a steady
rhythm and of meeting the absolute demand which is made
for a happy end. Curiously enough we seem to have little
difficulty in supplying it in the case of very young children,
but as they grow up we begin to question ourselves and to
wonder whether it is legitimate to declare that human lives
always do have happy endings. In one sense they quite obviously do not, but unless we can discover some sense in
which happiness can be legitimately affirmed, we shall find
ourselves not only depressed by Popper's "poverty of his-
toricism" but having to confess that all life is meaningless.
Then the past has no significance, then history is indeed
'bunk'.

In his book *Cosmos and History* already mentioned in

Chapter I Eliade demonstrates a strange, strong tendency for human beings to transform what he calls 'concrete' time into 'sacred' time, myth into history.

"Just before the last war (1939-45), the Romanian folklorist Constantin Brailoiu had occasion to record an admirable ballad in a village in Maramures. Its subject was a tragedy of love: the young suitor had been bewitched by a mountain fairy, and a few days before he was to be married, the fairy, driven by jealousy, had flung him from a cliff. The next day, shepherds found his body and, caught in a tree, his hat. They carried the body back to the village and his fiancee came to meet them; upon seeing her lover dead, she poured out a funeral lament, full of mythological allusions, a liturgical text of rustic beauty. Such was the content of the ballad. In the course of recording the variants that he was able to collect, the folklorist tried to learn the period when the tragedy had occurred; he was told that it was a very old story, which had happened 'long ago'. Pursuing his inquiries, however, he learned that the event had taken place not quite forty years earlier. He finally even discovered that the heroine was still alive. He went to see her and heard the story from her own lips. It was a quite commonplace tragedy: one evening her lover had slipped and fallen over a cliff; he had not died instantly; his cries had been heard by mountaineers; he had been carried to the village, where he had died soon after. At the funeral, his fiancee, with the other women of the village, had repeated the customary ritual lamentations, without the slightest allusion to the mountain fairy.

"Thus, despite the presence of the principal witness, a few years had sufficed to strip the event of all historical authenticity, to transform it into a legendary tale: the jealous fairy, the murder of the young man, the discovery of the dead body, the lament, rich in mythological themes, chanted by the fiancee. Almost all the people of the village had been contemporaries of the authentic historical fact; but this fact, as such, could not satisfy them: the tragic death of the young man on the eve of his marriage was something different from a simple death by accident; it had an occult meaning that could only be revealed by its identification with the category of myth. The mythicisation of the accident had not stopped at the creation of a ballad; people told the story of the jealous fairy even when they were talking freely, 'prosaically', of the young man's death. When the folklorist drew the villagers' attention to the authentic version, they replied that the old woman had forgotten; that her great grief had almost destroyed her mind. It was the myth that told the truth: the real story was already a falsification. Besides, was not the myth truer by the fact that it made the real story yield a deeper and richer meaning, revealing a tragic destiny?"[10]

Now an analogous tendency is to be discerned in children and immature adults: they too tend to generalise, to merge the particular into the general, to approximate the individual to the collective, the idea to the archetype. To the infant, for instance, eight months ago is simply a long time ago. It is a key task of education to train the child in learning how to offer appropriate resistance in due course to this necessarily anti-conscious, anti-cultural movement. The one vital mistake is to ask too much of him too soon, especially as the events which he experiences in concrete time consist not merely of "nice" things but increasingly and maybe preponderantly of "nasty" things. For quite a considerable period of his childhood it must be regarded as legitimate for him to deal with the present by projecting it into the past, but adolescence and maturity can only occur if the growing human organism is able to discriminate between the two kinds of time, giving each their due without either taking flight into mythical time, when he is airy-fairy and fantastic and divorced from daily life, or becoming petrified in concrete time, when he may at first claim to be the upholder of realism, the explainer away who is always ready to argue that "this is nothing but", yet who before long is consumed by an intellectual and spiritual nihilism. Early training in a true relationship to the past can do much to ensure that he avoids both these pitfalls.

All this means that we must reckon with an inability among young children to retain anything but archetypes: in crude language, Old Mother Hubbard, Queen Elizabeth I and Queen Victoria are the same image, and they can only gradually be distinguished as the child's own developing personality permits of life being lived individually as distinct from collectively. As we have already seen, this truth is admitted in the "lap situation", and the conventions of learning through story-telling are pretty widely recognised. It is at the next stage, and more and more quickly in succeeding ones, that such wisdom is neglected with the most dire consequences.

During the infant years, say up to seven, the educational use of myth and legend seems to require no further justification: the young child's tender, immature conscious apprehends the manifest content of the material, his large unconscious battens on the latent significance, and his education proceeds along the diagonal between the two. That the cultural diet offered must be large and varied is quite obvious from the tremendous variety of needs of the myriad psychological types of children, each of which needs appropriate objects in myth and legend on which to project his own as yet unconscious elements as a necessary stage towards their eventual introjection. The most basic case cf all will serve as sufficient example, namely that of the young child and his mother. Towards her he harbours the deepest ambivalent feeling of love and hate, both in her individual and archetypal capacity. In order that he may come to terms with these he requires a plentiful supply of feminine object images ranging along the psychological continuum from the witch to the madonna, in order that these can act as containers of his unconscious and therefore otherwise unmanageable libido. Only very slowly can he be expected to discriminate and to accept the first law of adulthood, namely that mother is neither witch nor madonna, but a human being like himself.

Over fifty years ago there appeared in a series of books called *Stories Old and New* a volume entitled *Tales of an Old Yew Tree* by Hugh Laurence.[11]

On the first printed page of this book, opposite to the beginning of Chapter One, there is printed the following factual statement.

The Darley Yew

"Whatever may be the exact age of this tree, there can be little doubt that it has given shelter to the Britons when planning the construction of the dwellings which they created not many yards to the west of its trunk; to the Romans who built up the funeral pyre to their slain comrades

*just clear of its branches; to the Saxons, converted, per-
chance, to the true faith by Bishop Dicima beneath its pleasant shade; to the Norman masons chiselling their quiet
sculptures to form the first stone house of prayer erected in
its vicinity; and to the host of Christian worshippers who,
from that day to this have been borne under hoary limbs in
women's arms to the baptismal font, and then on men's
shoulders to their last resting place, in soil that gave it birth."*

(Cox's Churches of Derbyshire)

The story begins by describing how two children, Harry
and Edith, go to stay for the holidays with their aunt and
uncle in Darley Dale in Derbyshire. Harry is presented with a
bow and arrows as a present and is eager to start shooting
them, but his Uncle John tells him to wait until the next
morning and spends the evening telling them stories about
great deeds that were done with bows and arrows long ago. "I
never see a bowman in these days, but I dare say they was
common enough in the dale here once upon a time." The two
children set out the next day into the countryside, and
Harry, experimenting with his bow, shoots an arrow right
into a thick old yew tree. When looking for it among the
branches, which they have climbed they encounter a "little
man dressed in green", who is tugging Harry's arrow out of
the bark of the tree for him. "Why, it hasn't even got a
point," he said, feeling the blunt brass tip with his tiny
brown fingers.

"It's only a toy bow and arrows," said Harry, who had
found his tongue now that the little man seemed so friendly.
"We were hunting for bears in the field yonder, and I shot
my arrow too far. That big stone over there was the bear."

"A good thing it weren't a real bear!" said the little green
man, with a funny grunt that was meant for a laugh. "Many
an adventure I've seen about here, which would have needed
good sharp arrows, aye and spears too."

"Do tell us about it," said Edith, who had quite got over
her awe at the little green man. For the next twenty chapters
or so he does just this, as the children visit him daily, stories
covering the Druids, the Romans, King Arthur, the early
Christian missionaries, the Danes, the Normans, Robin Hood,
Richard Coeur de Lion, the Battle of Bannockburn, Dick

Whittington, William Caxton, Mary Queen of Scots, the Civil War, Bonnie Prince Charlie, the first cotton mill and Florence Nightingale. The holidays come to an end, so Harry and Edith have to say goodbye to the little green man.

"You will be here next year if we come back again, won't you?" said Edith as they were leaving. The little man laughed.

"I've been here two thousand years," he said. "I'll not go away in a hurry now . . ."

"I wonder," said Harry in the train, "if some day, long after this, the little man will tell about the boy and girl who used to climb into his tree once upon a time to hear stories."

The above summary should suffice to indicate how this bit of story-telling really succeeds in initiating the two children into a significant relationship with the past. Here there is a perfect blending of fact and fantasy, a harmonious play between concrete time and mythological time, between historical events and archetypal phenomena. The riches of the latter are enormous: the little green man himself, primordial image of the ever-recurring renewal of life — "I've been here two thousand years — I'll not go away in a hurry now" — the Darley Yew, itself symbolic of the tree of life, with the children clambering up on the diagonals of its branches, impelled thither by the shot arrow of the questing young ego, and behind all the adventure of personality and history, which the children experience, is the containing safety of everyday Aunt Mary and Uncle John.

There have always been both constants and variables in the nature of the homes from which children come to school. The latter can be accounted for in many different ways — class character, urban or rural and so on — but it is the former which need special attention here. In any kind of homogeneous society these constants are explicitly stated and expressed by the few and implicitly accepted and assumed by the many, for example, the religious, political, aesthetic and sexual constants of medieval Europe or fifth-century Athens in their heyday. Where, however, the society lacks homogeneity, the constants disappear from the scene, that is to say they sink beneath the level of consciousness, thus permitting a situation to arise of moral, metaphysical and economic relativism where "anyone's guess is as good as anyone else's" — or so it seems. There are no consciously held and generally accepted absolute constants. Yet in reality the constants do persist, but at a much more primitive, instinctual, mass level, which sophisticated or pseudo-sophisticated minds ignore. This means that more and more the variables are noticed and debated and families are split on all kinds of questions dealing with manners, diet and sex. Then with alarming suddenness these are periodically exploded by the release of primitive constants, which bewilder and confuse because they seem to have nothing to do with the outward pattern of home life. How often the cry is heard about some young delinquent: "How could he have done such a thing, coming from a good home like his!"

Children coming to school must therefore be thought of, so far as non-totalitarian countries are concerned, as the products of a non-homogeneous society. In it there are many known variables and largely unknown, unrealised because unconscious constants, which when they manifest themselves tend to do so in an unconventional fashion. In the context of contemporary Western society it is the constants of Christian civilisation which for all but a minority have most obviously vanished, and this shows itself in the hardly disputable fact that homes seem to have little or no use for the Christian canon as it applies to the conduct of daily life.

In the face of such a situation schools can and do react in various ways. Some will try to counter the home situation by imposing on the child a firm traditional code of constants and regarding him as a success if he comes to accept them and a failure if he does not. A few others (the so-called progressive schools) will offer him more or less persuasively alternative constants of a variety of types, and some of these may commend themselves to some children, especially those whose parents themselves happen to be either violently for or against the particular school policy. Yet by far the most frequent reaction of the schools is merely to echo the non-homogeneity of society and the lack of constants in homes. This is shown by the absence of concerted policy among the staff, the atomisation of the curriculum, the disconnected specialisms and the steadily increasing drift towards collective repression by frightened adults of impatient adolescents in the sphere of social behaviour.

One of the most delicate situations between parents and

children arises when a child leaves home and goes to school for the first time, and discovers that there is a change of and increase in the outside authority figures. Instead of these being merely Mum and Dad, aunt, grandmother, and so on, Mr Jones and Miss Smith, the primary school teachers are added to them. In many ways of course they will be doing and saying most of the things that the family authority figures at home do and say, and so far as this is so they will be equally acceptable or unacceptable. But in other ways they will be behaving quite differently and so wielding a new kind of authority which each young child must learn to accept more or less readily.

Sometimes these two kinds of authority will conflict with one another: teacher says one thing and Mum another, and this presents the young child with what can be a most agonising conflict and what even in the most harmonious situation is bound to be a testing choice. Consider for a moment the full implications of the experience. The child is being asked to come to terms with the truth that home and parents do not have all the answers, that school and teachers have different ones. To which are they to be loyal? It is not always easy to behave loyally to both, and yet that is what seems to be expected of him.

A further complicating factor in the school situation is of course that the teacher has to perform this authority function not for one or two or three children in a family but for thirty or forty in a class. This means that it is bound to be a pretty rough and ready kind of authority, so that inevitably different types of children will in different ways experience the extremes of justice and injustice. From the age of infant school onwards the authority problem tends to revolve around two matters, one to do with behaviour and the other with knowledge. Although they must be discussed separately, they are of course closely intertwined and are part of the already complex entanglement of relationships between the personalities involved in the home and school scene.

As regards behaviour the authority problem arises in these kinds of way. At home "naughtiness", such as messing up the furniture or the food, may be seriously or leniently dealt with; at school it may be dealt with in exactly the same or exactly the opposite way. This means that the adult authority expressing either attitude is bound very often to vary, and the child therefore quite justly concludes that either Mum or Miss Smith is not "being fair". Or again, at school silence may be regarded as a virtue, while at home it is regarded as a vice. At home Dad may reason gently with Johnny while at school Mr Jones may roar loudly at him; nowadays it is most likely to be the other way round. At home it may be quite the thing to answer back gaily when reprimanded, while at school the polite assent is what is demanded.

Nowadays too there is far more likelihood of division between authority patterns in home and school, because in the wider society which both reflect there is so little general agreement about the source and nature of authority. Obviously, when school and home speak with the same voice, at any rate on most things, the pattern of behaviour development is smoother than when they do not. But even so no child can avoid having to respond to differing and often contradictory voices of authority, and he will not be free of this conflict until he has grown his own inside authority for himself.

It will be argued here that the history of homes, studied in a suitable philosophical framework, could help to solve this problem. How? By furnishing teachers and pupils with the wherewithall to rediscover constants on a new level of consciousness and so bring order into the existing confusion of the variables.

Between the ages of eleven and thirteen many children are reaching the end of the first stage of their journey away from home and origins and starting out on a second stage of encounters. For now they emerge definitively from the parental shell and begin to peck about more boldly on their own at the scraps of information which their expanding horizon reveals. One of the most obvious of these is the fact that not all homes are alike. As a fact of empirical experience each young boy and girl discovers that his neighbour's circumstances do not altogether correspond to his own. Because they are different he will more often than not regard them as inferior to his own, though frequently he may learn of things which he envies in them and wishes he had in his own. It is from this springboard of the growing point of interest of the child that the teacher can invite a dive into the manifest content of the subject. In selecting that material he should be guided by the following considerations, which derive from his realisation of its latent significance. In the first place there will be the prevailing patterns of family life, constellated by the relationships of mother and father to each other and of the child to his parents. As already suggested, these must be expected to vary widely from the conventional, rigid and traditional to the almost incoherently formless and rootless. In almost all cases there will exist a need among these young boys and girls now approaching puberty to secure a coherence in their new life, a "reassuring liaison" between it and the family. Jung has explained the psychological aspect of this two-way stretch with reference to the destiny of the individual:

". . . leaving the mother, the source of life, behind him, he is driven by an unconscious desire to find her again, to return to her womb. Every obstacle that rises in his path and hampers his ascent wears the shadowy features of the Terrible Mother, who saps his strength with the poison of secret doubt and retrospective longing, and in every conquest he wins back again his smiling, love and life giving mother."[12]

In another passage Jung underlines this truth with some further elucidation:

"The remnants of the child-soul in the adult make kings or pawns of the insignificant figures who move about on the checkerboard of life, turning some poor devil of a casual father into a ferocious tyrant, or a silly goose of an unwilling mother into a goddess of fate. For behind every individual father there stands the primordial image of the Father and behind the fleeting personal mother the magical figure of the Magna Mater. These archetypes of the collective unconscious, whose power is magnified in immortal works of art and in the fiery tenets of religion, are the dominants that rule the pre-conscious soul of the child, and, when projected upon the human parents, lend them a fascination which often assumes monstrous proportions."[13]

There are four main ingredients in the educational situation of the child: his relationship to his own actual parents, his relationship to the archetypal parental projections which they hold for him, his relationship to his teachers, who will play a complex mixture of both these roles, and finally his relationship to the various parental figures appearing by deliberate choice of the educator in the manifest content of his social studies syllabus. It is through a harmonious blending of these four that the teacher can teach and the pupil can learn. Erich Neumann has well summarised the crucial importance of this achievement in the following words: "The integration of personal psychic phenomena with the corresponding trans-personal symbols is of paramount importance for the further development of consciousness and for the synthesis of personality."[14]

What are the images then that we have of:

1   The kind of dwellings we inhabit? Who built them? What they are made of? Whether they suit primitive man or whether his will suit us?

2   The size of our families? Are we typical with say an average of two or three children to each household? Are our parents different at all, a little or a lot from the parents of primitive man?

3   What our parents work at? Do they work at home, nearby or far away? Do they all earn the same money, or are some richer than others, and how does this compare with primitive man?

4   The difference between work and play? Are our games at all like those of primitive man? What kind of schooling did he and do we have? Which is the more effective?

5   The things which we value most in life — our parents, our pocket money, our health or what, and how does this compare with what we have discovered about the values of primitive man? Are some values the same everywhere and always, or are they simply a matter of custom, chance, climate?

The key questions that require educational answers in the context of learning are first, how far has the child personally come to terms with the image of his own home and sense of origin, and secondly how far is this image globally valid for people of all nations?

3

The Theme of Conflict in Education

"He that wrestles with us strengthens our nerves and sharpens our skill. Our antagonist is our helper."

Burke

Boys and girls all over the world are faced with the same experience at puberty, however variable may be the context in which it occurs. This is when their now rapidly developing egos become acutely aware of conflict: they encounter a division between 'I' and 'not-I' on an alarmingly increased scale, they feel themselves caught in a network of contradictions. A much deeper understanding than ever before of the psychology of this condition, its superficial variants and fundamental similarity, combined with the demands of global unification, now make it both imperative and possible to devise and practise an education for adolescent years equally valid in all parts of the earth. This can revolve around the parallel and related processes of the typical hero career as depicted in history and the typical growth of the ego as evidenced in individual personality. Erik H. Erikson remarks in his book *Identity. Youth and Crisis:*[1] "we deal with a process 'located' in the core of the individual and yet also in the core of his communal culture, a process which established, in fact, the identity of those two identities." (p.22) "Nor can we separate (as I tried to demonstrate in Young Man Luther) the identity crisis in individual life and contemporary crises in historical development because the two help to define each other and are truly relative to each other." (p.23)

It is in terms of Hero and Ego, Adversary and 'Shadow' that I shall now try to discuss the truth springing from the creative relationship between them. We need to remember that the urge to heroism and adventure, although deeply present in children always, receives fairly constant repression in twentieth-century urban life and that an adventurous timetable can offer some outlet for it, if skilfully devised.

The essence of the argument lies in the fact that every tale of the hero in myth and history represents in sequential, projected form the emergence of the ego in personality: the hero essays to 'break the cake of custom', the ego to win some degree of independence of the unconscious. As Neumann has demonstrated, "the stages of the hero myth have become constituent elements in the personal development of every individual."[2]

Just as there are evidently different types of hero, so there are obviously different types of ego; the main distinction lies between the extrovert and the introvert, between the adventurer, the leader, the liberator or the freely outward-going ego, and on the other hand the culture bearer, the dreamer and saviour of the inward-turning ego. Strung out along the extended line which joins these two extremes is every conceivable kind of mixture of them both, and these are of course also personified in the individual pupils of a school class. Thus the kinds of heroism which will commend themselves are bound to vary enormously, even to that strangely fascinating point where A denies that B's hero is a hero at all yet hesitates to label him a villain. Two things however are clear enough, namely that heroic images must be sufficiently diverse to exercise some surface fascination on all human types, and that in due course the resistance they encounter, which is what gives them the opportunity to become heroes, will itself require some explanatory treatment.

A threefold rhythm seems to mark the hero's life and the ego's development, separation from native setting and parents, initiation into the dangerous adventure of overcoming an enemy, externally the dragon and internally the ever-present threat to the ego from the unconscious, and return with the won treasure of successful external achievement or internal ego independence. Now the process of transition by means of which the young person and the hero gain their respective emancipation from that on which they previously depended has traditionally and of necessity been marked by ritual and ceremony. For example there are the various rites of young males attaining puberty and the birth of secret societies and gangs at about this age. In contemporary Western society there is a deplorable poverty of such ritual in recognised and legitimate form; hence the many illegitimate forms which may and do appear as compensations.

"The death of ritual has led to the blocking of the outlet of the unconscious, the dark side of human understanding. . . . From the grossest beginnings in primitive religion there has always been some sense of the transcendental whole to which man could re-unite himself through ritual, and to which he could signal by the use of symbols. There is very little left of it at the moment. Our artists struggle, but it is hard for them; they are priests in an atheistic society."[3]

Teachers and parents would do well to ask themselves what version of the Indians' 'guardian spirit' can be made available to their own children requiring initiation. Baynes has pointed out the high importance of such a procedure:

"Each member of the Indian family is thus taught to meet the crucial phase and predictable transition in his life with the support of the correspondingly mythological stream or archetype. By this means an internal continuity is established between the primordial psyche and cultural development, and a 'reassuring liaison' established between individual consciousness and the mystic images of the racial unconscious."[4]

There could hardly be a more exact description of what must be the essential ingredient of the latent significance of our study material: it must be of such a kind as to provide the 'support of the corresponding mythological stream' — in this case the hero archetype. In this way the 'internal continuity' is procured and each one of us is helped to find and see himself, no longer either literally or symbolically a 'displaced person', but as playing an intelligible role within the human drama, linked to the past, poised in the present and ready to spring forward into the future.

"However well," continues Baynes, "the adolescent boy may succeed in this complex adaptation, the unconverted, infantile psyche still lies repressed, and potentially explosive, just beneath the fair, cultural surface. This ignored, primordial island presents a formidable educational problem to western society, which has so far remained singularly incapable of envisaging this vital problem of initiation either in education or religion."[5]

The way is hard and in the last resort not to be trodden to the end except by those who have at least begun to see the point of the resistances which hurt and seemingly hinder them. Before considering those, let us take some examples and see how their imagery can be utilised: they are selected from the scene of legend, because this is where education in encounter can most appropriately begin and also because it illustrates more obviously than does the historical scene the underlying unity of the problem.

The Primitive Hero

When? Where? How? Why? These four blunt interrogatives can satisfactorily be made the points of departure for the study of the heroes and their opponents. A start could be made with the hero of primitive societies. This would entail an elementary investigation of what is meant by the term primitive, that is, to which chronological age it may refer, and why it is that some near primitive societies are still extant in the twentieth century AD, separated by twenty thousand years from those which have become extinct. Location of such past and contemporary societies forms the beginning of an answer to the second question, where, and in the light of answers obtained to these queries of time and places there can next be presented the figure of the primitive hero. In what consisted his heroism? Essentially it was his desire and capacity 'to break the cake of custom' by some deed of moral, technical or merely physical skill. He was the man who dared to act differently, or to think differently and, so doing, provides us, like Hiawatha, with the story of

> . . . how he lived and toiled and suffered
> That the tribes of men might prosper
> That he might advance his people.[6]

Yet such action was and is always bound to provoke objection from the conservative majority elements in society: the innovator always risks failure if the task he has attempted is too great or destruction at the hands of critics if what he is striving for goes too much against the tradition of his people, if they are not yet ready for him. Then he is a hero, caught and destroyed by the future, instead of one who successfully mediates the future to his fellow-men through his own superior vision of it.

Some such theme provides the manifest content of this first stage of the history of conflict. As for its latent significance, Jung himself provides the relevant commentary:—

"The song of Hiawatha contains material that is well suited to bring into play the vast potentials for archetypal symbolisation latent in the human mind, and to stimulate the creation of images. But the products always contain the same old human problems, which rise again and again in new symbolic guise from the shadowy world of the unconscious."[7]

Four heroes of the legendary scene may be chosen from as wide a range as possible. The four I have selected for treatment here as examples spring from Judaistic, Greek, Romano-British and Teutonic sources.

The Judaistic Hero: Moses

When and where did he live? Round the crude answers of 'about 1300 BC in Egypt', there could be assembled a rich store of material, certain to fascinate by reason of its mixture of fantasy and realism. First there will be built up a picture of the land of Egypt under the pharaohs and of the tribes of Israel. The story of Joseph and his brethren could lead on to an account of the subject state of the Jews in Egypt as a necessary setting of the scene for the emergence of the saviour deliverer, Moses. From the beautiful biblical account of his discovery in the bullrushes of the Nile and his subsequent promotion to the highest office of Pharaoh's court could arise the question of its historical veracity. Did it really happen like that? If not, what is the true gist of the story? Then could follow the story of Exodus, the wanderings in the wilderness with the climax of Moses's vision of the promised land. The opportunity could and should be taken to link this ancient piece of history with the twentieth-century creation of the state of Israel and, above all, there would arise the challenge of wherein lay the inspiration which gave this particular hero his dynamic. Was it his conviction of his unique relationship to the one true God of the Jews, Jehovah? Was it this that gave him power and authority? How does this kind of belief compare and contrast with the trust in many gods? As regards educational method, this particular hero story obviously lends itself readily to dramatic treatment and also affords opportunities for the practice of the painting and modelling arts: the Nile, the Pyramids, the Sphinx, Mount Sinai, and, above all, each child's own version of the promised land. Then again it is easy enough to present the other side, the forces against which Moses had to struggle, the minority striving to assert its right to existence against the majority, the intractable perils and vicissitudes of the actual journey out of Egypt. Of the latent significance of the Moses story it is enough to refer to Michelangelo's massive presentation of the hero.

The Greek Hero: Odysseus

A wealth of attractive source material suggests itself immediately for the manifest content of our next hero study, that of Odysseus. Answers to the when, where and how questions can be culled from Homer and from the most reliable evidences of archaeology. The journey from Ithaca to Troy and back again can be presented in brilliant colours and made the occasion for a whole series of adventurous encounters between the hero and his adversaries, whether human or supernatural. It is with the latent significance of the Odysseus theme that we may occupy ourselves here, and especially with the appeal which this deeper level will be having to the unconscious layers of our personalities. This example should indeed provide us with a first-class instance of the way of looking at history as a projection of the collective past in the psyche. It is a supreme example of the truth that "our identity with the fleeting consciousness of the present is, however, so great that we forget the timelessness of our psychic foundations"[8] — unless, that is, the relationship between our personality and history becomes an integrated one. We should begin by recognising the classic, archetypal pattern of the hero's career. First there is the separation of Odysseus from family and home to go abroad and perform warrior deeds "far on the ringing plains of windy Troy". Secondly, there is his initiation as a skilful general and then as a harassed traveller, but though his "bark be tempest tossed" it cannot be lost. We may reflect in passing on the meaning of Poseidon's fury against Odysseus, that is, a symbolic presentation of the menacing sea-mother motif, and also on the roles of Circe and Nausicaa as contrasting aspects of the Jungian anima archetype. Then again we may note the significant hint put into the mouth of the goddess Athene (*Odyssey,* Book 13) about the real heroism of Odysseus, namely, daring to be different, to essay a new venture in consciousness: "How like you," she says to him, "to be so wary. And that is why I cannot desert you in your misfortunes; you are so civilised, so independent, so self-possessed."

Thirdly there is the hero's return, his homecoming to the familiar dog, shepherd, nurse, father and wife, followed by the climax of his heroism, the conflict with Penelope's suitors and their slaughter: he has defeated his enemies both external and domestic. It is a barbaric revenge but one in keeping with the modes of that day and — the question might be raised — not unknown today after a lapse of two thousand years.

Why is it that this three-stage Odyssey has continued to appeal to every succeeding generation of man, with the character of the hero being modelled to suit the needs of the times? Because, of course, the story symbolises man's eternal quest for the meaning of things, his voyages of discovery into the nature of the universe and his own part in it. Odysseus appears at sundry times in classical or romantic guise, as a tough and cunning politician and as a romantic wanderer. In Shakespeare's *Troilus and Cressida* he is the hero of 'order':

> How could communities,
> Degrees in schools and brotherhoods in cities,
> Peaceful commerce from dividable shores,
> The primogenitive and due of birth,
> Prerogative of age, crowns, sceptres, laurels,
> But by degree, stand in authentic place,
> Take but degree away, untune that string,
> And hark, what discord follows.
>   (Act I, Scene iii)

Professor Stanford has collected the evidence which shows how Odysseus has appeared successively as sixth-century BC opportunist, fifth-century BC sophist or demagogue, fourth-century BC Stoic, medieval baron, learned clerk or pre-Columbian explorer, as seventeenth-century prince or politician, eighteenth-century philosopher or primal man, nineteenth-century disillusioned aesthete and twentieth-century proto-Fascist and "humble citizen of Megapolis".[9] Kazantzakis' epic poem is entitled *The Odyssey — a Modern Sequel*[10] and it is probably the greatest recent testimony to the constancy and enduring relevance of the theme. This 'man of many turns' raises excellently the question of what constitutes heroism in history and personality and what is the nature of the resistance requisite to produce it. The Trojans and the Greeks, the natural elements and the pressing suitors were all sounding-boards of Odysseus' prowess. In psychological terms this means the bold essay of the ego towards independence, the desire for novelty and experiment, some capacity to bring it about, and the ability to cope with its often crucial consequences for the hero and for the adolescent.

King Arthur

Our third suggestion, the hero warrior, King Arthur, is a semi-legendary character but definitely more historical than Odysseus. For all Europeans his story is a particularly apt and attractive one at the level of manifest content. The scene is laid in sixth-century Britain after the main departure of the Roman occupiers; it is peopled by a soldier of the West and his followers, who are engaged in fighting various new brands of invaders. Who exactly was this *"Dux Bellorum Dux Brittaniarum"*? How far was he in Ramsay's words "a hero of romance, a pure myth"? How can we get at him, this *'ursus horribilis'*, through later literary accretions such as Mallory's "Morte d'Arthur" and Tennyson's "Idylls of the King"?

To begin with, the symbol of the cup and the sword and the entire archetypal mystery of the Holy Grail legend need to be appreciated implicitly if not expressed explicitly, carefully avoiding any trace of sentimentality. Indeed we shall do well to ponder the earliest expressions of the Grail motif in ancient fertility rites and the Egyptian vessel that acted as Sun-catcher. These and the Mithras-Attis cults underlie the Christian symbolism, and their recognition gives even greater weight to the traditional aim of the quest for the Holy Grail, namely to benefit the King (the Fisherman, the ego who goes out to fish) and to restore the waste land, to be the traditional saviour of the land and its people.

> I sat upon the shore
> Fishing, with the arid plain behind me
> Shall I at least set my lands in order?
> London Bridge is falling down falling down
>   falling down.[11]

This is the manner in which a poet can help us savour the "timeless moment" of that connection.

The archetypal pattern of King Arthur's career, so far as it may be surmised, is clear enough: first, separation in the sense of departing from the prevailing attitude of defeatism and rallying his countrymen against the invader, secondly initiation of a truly military character into a series of mighty battles, and thirdly return to Avalon, to the tomb and womb of the unconscious, all complete with the familiar tradition that he would return to his country's aid in the darkest hour of her need. To this level of interpretation of his life's journey may be added that of the perennial journey of man in search of his soul, of wholeness, of the Grail for which the knights of the Round Table were searching. The fact that, like St George, King Arthur has become a popular national hero in Britain and has been and still is the object of much artistic attention in music, poetry and painting, suggests that there is a great deal in the manifest content of his tale which will appeal to a wide variety of types. Knightly deed and savage plot, courtly love and blinding lust, wickedness and innocence, the pagan-Christian blending of human qualities, all these undoubtedly set off reverberations in our unconscious.

The Siegfried Legend

A fourth possible suggestion from the legendary scene, which certainly belongs to the European cultural tradition, is the Nibelungen Lied. Its stark elemental theme stands in startling contrast to the Arthurian one. Also the fact that, written in the later Middle Ages, it obviously refers to a much earlier period in nordic history and mythology and that it has forward relevance as well to the Hitler phenomenon of the twentieth century, adds to its probably manifest appeal. (See Chapter VIII.) The characters of Siegfried the hero and Hagen his shadow make a significant example of the encounter of opposites, and once again from the vantage point of our bridge across time, the past and present illuminate each other, as the following quotation makes clear:

"The youth in Hitler's Germany, who had been taught to identify with a Siegfried ideal, to look upon himself as a budding superman (and so to lose all contact with his own reality), who had learnt to project everything that was vile in himself upon the 'race-enemy': when that 'race-enemy' fell within his power, was all too liable to become wholly possessed by a demonic shadow – with what results the concentration camps revealed. And what was true of German youth, since the necessary means of conditioning (both ability to condition and readiness to be conditioned) can be true of any other people, not excluding ourselves."[12]

Enough has been said by way of illustrating how the heroic images of the legendary scene can nourish us.

Outward and Inward Conflict

Experience of frustration and opposition will be a daily, a familiar, if often resented, experience: conflict among our peers, with the other gang, the other set, conflict with the parents (the indignant "Surely I'm old enough now"), conflict with teachers ("Sir, it's not fair"), and above all conflict within ourselves. By this last is meant the heroic, often foolhardy and pathetic assertion of the ego against the conventional demands of society when it strives to be true to itself. Our diet must therefore consist of the dark to balance the light, the dragon to challenge St George, evil to give countenance to good. It must consist of evidence to convince us that, as Simone Weil expresses it, "Evil is the shadow of good. A real good, endowed with solidarity and density, projects evil. It is only imaginary good, which does not project evil."[13] With even greater philosophical brevity, she adds: "the existence of evil is the fault of the good." That should be our basic introduction to the stubborn fact of destiny, namely that in tossing up the coin of life, whether we call heads or tails, we cannot take away the one side without the other.

> For this is Destiny: being opposite
> And nothing else, and always opposite.[14]

This way of looking at things can only proceed from a proper understanding of the role of evil in human affairs and the nature of its personification in the figure of the devil. It is perhaps helpful to conceive of him as originating in early man's projection of everything that he regarded as threatening his sense of security and personal identity on to some external object. As soon in fact as he became detached from his original state of identification and 'participation mystique', man became aware of the perils of his new condition as represented for example by the hazards of nature (see Chapter II). Everything that was not himself had to be seen as his not-self, his opposite, and as a most deadly enemy when it threatened to destroy his tender young ego; hence, animism and the need to propitiate gods or devils; hence also the dualist mysteries of the Orient, Mara in Indian thought for the wicked one, Yang and Yin in Chinese philosophy, the legend of Ormuzd and Ahrimane, taken up by Israel during the Babylonian captivity, and the emergence of the figure of Satan, a Semitic word meaning to oppose.

In Rabbinical literature there is present the idea of Satan as the 'evil impulse' in man, an essential part even of God's creation. Then the themes of the symbolic role of the serpent, the change from Lucifer, Bringer of Light, to the Prince of Darkness, the Accuser, lead on to a consideration of the Christian treatment of the devil figure. Why did the Council of Constantinople in AD 547 declare him eternal? How correct was Anselm in posing the "problem of the existence of evil in an universe supposedly made and controlled by a good and loving God"? What happened to the devil in post-Reformation times in Europe, in the 'Age of Enlightenment', in the climate of nineteenth-century secularism? As long ago as the 1910 edition of the *Encyclopaedia Britannica* the following statement appeared in the article on the Devil (Volume VIII): "it may be confidently affirmed that belief in Satan is not now generally regarded as an essential article of the Christian faith, nor is it found to be an indispensable element of Christian experience."

Is this, one wonders, acceptable doctrine in contemporary Christian apologetics? Is it pertinent to the experiences of Western man between 1910 and 1970? Is the 'little gentleman' of Ivan in *The Brothers Karamazov* an 'objective reality or the projection of the unadmitted elements in his soul'? "Well," says the devil in André Gide's *The Counterfeiters,* "why are you scared of me? You know very well I don't exist." "The Devil's cleverest wile," wrote Baudelaire in his 'Short Prose Poems', "Is to convince us that he does not exist."[15] Some of these considerations might be in the background of the teacher's mind as he presents his material historically: its psychological import will now be examined. Central to it is the concept of the 'shadow' as developed by Jung.

"I think it will help you to understand the term 'shadow'," he writes, "if you consider first its relation to the Ego. Shadow implies that there is a source of light in front of your body which casts a shadow behind you. The source of light is consciousness. Consciousness like light casts a shadow. Always that function which is behind you, depending where the light is, is in the shadow."[16]

There is the personal, individual 'shadow', a man's 'inferior function', consisting of that which the conscious position deprecates, his mortal enemy, his *'bête noire'*, the side of himself which, when he recognises it, he dislikes and which is generally repressed but apt to erupt when its opposite in consciousness is too far stretched. There is also the archetypal 'shadow', an 'autonomous complex', of the collective unconscious, related to the other archetypes, having to do with man's instinctual, animal ancestry. It is through learning to recognise 'shadow' phenomena, that access is obtained, as through a dark and dangerous gateway, to the Unconscious and so eventually to the Self or core of human totality. "Nobody is whole without negative qualities,"[17] and the process of education consists to a great extent in the progressive recognition and coming to terms with that negative quality.

What are its symptoms? It is a frequent element in the

imagery of dreams, a literary phenomenon, for example Falstaff as Henry V's shadow, Caliban as Prospero's ("this thing of darkness I acknowledge mine"), Nietzsche's 'Ugliest man', Mr Hyde to Dr Jekyll. Its social aspect can be seen in the army of the 'enemy', the rival business concern or the character of the school 'cad'. It is the 'intrusive spirit', often manifested as naughtiness in a child's psyche and behaviour, which themselves are carrying the unrecognised and un-acknowledged unresolved problems of the parents, namely their 'shadows'. Of course, as with all archetypal situations, there is always a hook in the conscious position for the archetype to hang on: the enemy is in truth partly evil, the cad is in truth to some degree despicable, the child is in truth partly a 'bundle of mischief'.

Perhaps man's greatest 'shadow' has always been what is called death, for it is "the primordial symbol of the decay and dissolution of the personality".[18] It is the greatest threat to the conscious position, and one which is bound sooner or later to prevail as long as consciousness is ego-centred and not, in the Jungian sense, 'self-centred'. The shadow of death can only be tolerated from the standpoint of totality, from what Rilke called 'the other side of life'. "Stability and indestructibility, the true goals of centroversion have their mythological prototype in the conquest of death, in man's defences against its power."[19] The 'shadow' is that which appears to constitute a threat to our sense of personal identity and yet is that from which identity alone derives.

Good, God, security, wholeness can only be consciously realised by means of their opposites, evil, the devil, insecurity. To know at all, we have to know what we would not know. To learn at all, we have to learn the bitter with the sweet.

Enough has been said by now to indicate the main lines on which our understanding of the latent significance of the phenomenon of conflict should be running. Aided by such insights, we are now in a position to select the manifest content of such material as deals with the "hero with a thousand faces"[20] and the spirit that in Goethe's Faust "for ever denies".

In suggesting the following historical figures as images for analysis, I have adopted a double criterion. In the first place I have selected them because they are germane to and can be seen to be germane to the story of Western civilisation; other civilisations could and undoubtedly would select different figures. In the second place they correspond exactly to the demands for a connection between manifest content and latent significance, which we are constantly making. It would seem sensible to select our manifest material of conflict from the five great social upheavals of modern history, the English Revolution of the seventeenth century, the French Revolution of the eighteenth century, the Russian Revolution of the twentieth century, the establishment of American unity and independence in the nineteenth century and the similar establishment of Indian or Chinese unity and independence in the twentieth century.

The manifest content of the imagery for each of the revolutionary heroes could be conveniently gathered under the same four headings of when, where, how and why.

The English Revolution: Oliver Cromwell

In the case of the first of these, Oliver Cromwell, the chronological question should be answered generally and specifically, that is to say, the seventeenth century and the dates of his personal life span (1599-1658). The geographical and environmental question should also be answered generally and specifically: the British Isles and Europe and especially the Eastern counties and Westminster. To the third question of why Oliver Cromwell trod the stage of human affairs with such prominence, an answer should gradually be built up in two terms, one pertaining to his own unique personality, the other to the state of consciousness reigning in Western society some three hundred years ago. How this was an amalgam of conflicting political, economic and spiritual factors, often operating in antithesis to one another, could be graphically illustrated by means of examples of conflict as it was expressed at the Stuart Court and in the House of Commons, at Naseby and Drogheda, between Roundhead and Cavalier, in the struggle for the reclamation of the Fenlands and above all in the heart and mind of the man, Cromwell, himself. As John Middleton Murry wrote splendidly about Oliver's self-questioning speeches: "to me, as to Carlyle long before me, these knotted, sinewy wrestling speeches of the Lord Protector are very wonderful. In them one feels the dumb creative force of life striving for utterance, striving to say things that cannot be said; the great instrument of becoming, struggling to make comprehensible to man the necessity that was upon him . . ."[21] The "cruel necessity" of King Charles I's execution could well provide the pivot which should provide the answer to the fourth question of how. The final lesson which should emerge is that in this revolutionary hero's career there may be found clues to a better understanding of some constant laws of human existence as exemplified in the Glorious Revolution. One is that advances and innovations in the consciousness of the collectivity are focused in the lives of outstanding individuals: the other is that each such revolutionary movement and the men and women in whom it is personified inevitably either suffer or enforce the reaction which the revolutionary impulse evokes.

The French Revolution: Napoleon

In the case of Napoleon Bonaparte the double answer to the question when, is the end of the eighteenth and the beginning of the nineteenth centuries and the period 1769-1821. The double answer to the question, where, is France, especially Paris, and then practically the whole of the rest of the civilised world! To the third question of why, the answers must again be built up in terms of the hero's own personality, not least his relationship with a fickle father and a *"Maitresse Mère"* and also in terms of the many-tiered conflict raging in French society during the reigns of Louis XV and Louis XVI. Both for this answer and for the answer to the question of how, no better text could be taken than Napoleon's own words: "We have done with the Romance of the Revolution: we must now commence its history."

What is meant by those words in the light of the Code Napoléon, of the bridge at Lodi, of the retreat from Moscow and the battle of Waterloo? Lessons occupied in seeking answers to this problem would again be concerned with the tense drama involved in all the different and conflicting claims of persons and groups for their own particular vision of truth. How well this could be illustrated through contemporary English writings about Bony and through French ones of *"le petit Caporal"*! How the deeper stops could be pulled out by introducing the class to that wonderful opening scene in Tolstoy's *War and Peace!*

"Well, Prince," says Anna Pavlovna to Prince Vassili in July 1805, "Genoa and Lucca are now nothing more than the appanages, than the private property of the Bonaparte family. I warn you that if you do not tell me we are going to have war, if you still allow yourself to condone all the infamies, all the atrocities of this anti-Christ — on my word I believe he is an anti-Christ — that is the end of our acquaintance."

The Russian Revolution: Lenin

Here the double answer to the question when, is the early part of the twentieth century and the period 1870-1924; to the second, where, Russia; to the third, why, first there is the reply in terms of Lenin's own character: "there is no one else who for the whole twenty-four hours of every day is busy with the Revolution, who thinks and even dreams only of the Revolution. What can you do with a man like that?" So writes one close to him.[22] Why was it that this dedicated soul or conversely this fanatical lunatic could forge and half succeed in realising his watchword, "Power to the Soviets, land to the peasants, bread to the starving and peace to all men"? The answer will need to be built up out of a growing knowledge of the background of Tsarist Russia, of terrorism, of Lenin's own years of exile, of his return to the Finland Station in 1917 to the bitter days of the Civil War, to the need for the N.E.P., to his own death and embalming. In finding answers to the question, how, plenty of material could be utilised to show wherein lay the spiritual, economic and political content of the ideological conflict. As with Napoleon Bonaparte, so with Lenin, attention should once again be drawn to the role of the outstanding individual in being the focus of an advance in collective consciousness and to the iron law which decrees that every revolution causes its reaction, which may wipe out all progress or which may spend its force before the newly gained objective is obliterated by its savage surge backwards.

These three hero figures conform of course to the traditional pattern of separation, initiation and return: an image which advances finally to the forefront of our consciousness. Cromwell was separated from these of his countrymen and class, who were unwilling or unable to do anything about the Stuart despotism; he was initiated into the conflict of debate and battle; he returned to struggle unsuccessfully with the task of establishing new forms of order out of the disruption of the kingdom. Napoleon was separated from his Corsican origins, initiated into the revolutionary wars, returned "to confirm the Revolution" but even in the hour of partial success suffered personal defeat and eclipse. Lenin was separated from the ruling class of Tsarist Russia and from his early terrorist associates, was initiated into the Bolshevik struggle and returned to labour rather more successfully than either of the other two to establish new forms of order after the revolution.

The two other figures who might be selected from the historical scene are not quite the same kind of revolutionary heroes as the previous three. Each of them played a truly revolutionary role in their native countries and each had lasting influence on the whole world.

Lincoln: a Fusion of Sentiments

The nineteenth century and the years 1805-65 and particularly the United States north and south are the main answers to the first two relevant questions about the career of Abraham Lincoln. Once again, an answer to the why must be sought for in the individual character of the boy from the log cabin and even more in the head of consciousness which had gathered on the North American continent from so many different lands: a head accompanied in the southern states by the dark, heavy body of slavery. What Lincoln focused in his person was the tremendous fusion of the sentiment of American nationalism and Negro emancipation, together with all the powers favouring Secession which countered it, and of which the hero himself was the eventual victim. In working out the use of the story, every opportunity should be seized to connect Lincoln's career with the events of 1688, 1789 and 1776, and also of sketching however broadly the outlines of what has become one of the greatest problems of the contemporary world, namely that of colour. Increased consciousness of the rights of political and economic emancipation have brought with them, it could be shown, increased challenges in the shape of a demand for real human solidarity, irrespective of race or class or creed.

Gandhi

Let us switch our attention to a phenomenon of the twentieth century and especially of the years 1869-1948, which cover the life of Gandhi, and his effect on India, South Africa and the whole world. The question, why, must seek an answer in the strange, rich personality of a man who was half saint and half shrewd politician. It must be sought as well in the collective consciousness which seems to have emerged out of the encounter between an ancient civilisation, the Hindu religion and the British rule in India. The story of how, culminating in the tragic murder of the hero, could well bring out what seems to be a constant law of human behaviour, namely that the more violence there is in any great social upheaval, the less real revolution there is likely to be. To this could be added a consideration of the nature of non-violent resistance, both as practised by Gandhi and in its more universal application, possibly as the only alternative to suicide by means of nuclear fission and the only adequate response to totalitarianism.[23]

The Response to Totalitarianism

A final example is chosen deliberately from very recent history, with the idea of posing this great problem of society in the modern world, namely that of totalitarianism. Just because young people today are not old enough to remember the Second World War as part of their own conscious memory, it is all the more important that they should obtain some insight into this most tremendous of all social conflicts by means of an appraisal of the Hitler phenomenon (see Chapter VIII). The following passage provides an admirable piece of manifest content:

"In this age of unenlightened despotism Hitler has 'had more than a few rivals', yet he remains, so far, the most remarkable of those who have used modern technique to apply the classic formulas of tyranny.

"Before the war it was common to hear Hitler described as the pawn of the sinister interests who held real power in

Germany, of the Junkers or the Army, of heavy industry or high finance. This view does not survive examination of the evidence. Hitler acknowledged no masters, and by 1938 at least he exercised arbitrary rule over Germany to a degree rarely, if ever, equalled in a modern industrialised state.

"At the same time, from the re-militarisation of the Rhineland to the invasion of Russia, he won a series of successes in diplomacy and war which established an hegemony over the continent of Europe comparable with that of Napoleon at the height of his fame. While these could not have been won without a people and an Army willing to serve him, it was Hitler who provided the indispensable leadership, the flair for grasping opportunities, the boldness in using them. In retrospect his mistakes appear obvious, and it is easy to be complacent about the inevitability of his defeat: but it took the combined efforts of the three most powerful nations in the world to break his hold on Europe.

"Luck and the disunity of his opponents will account for much of Hitler's success — as it will of Napoleon's — but not for all. He began with few advantages, a man without a name and without support other than that which he acquired for himself, not even a citizen of the country he aspired to rule. To achieve what he did Hitler needed — and possessed — talents out of the ordinary which in sum amounted to political genius, however evil its fruits . . . Hitler indeed was a European, no less than a German phenomenon. The conditions and the state of mind which he exploited, the malaise of which he was the symptom, were not confined to one country, although they were more strongly marked in Germany than anywhere else. Hitler's idiom was German, but the thoughts and emotions to which he gave expression have a more universal currency."[24]

Here, within a German setting, three aspects of a contemporary tendency to social disease, which is more indeed than a purely German phenomenon may be observed. These are: first, the very nature of totalitarianism; secondly, the impossibility of it being resisted by traditional methods of statecraft, and thirdly, the need for a creative response to its challenge. This essentially democratic response must be such as to be capable of accepting the daemonic elements inherent in it and so by transcending them to pass beyond resistance.

It is necessary to distinguish clearly between totalitarianism and the various kinds of authoritarian dictatorships which have existed from time to time in history. The former is a modern phenomenon and is essentially of European origin. It is the expression first of the individually and collectively unsolved problem of the shadow, secondly of the rise to power of the pseudo-educated masses, and thirdly the rapid industrialisation and urbanisation of previously rural communities. It expresses the reaction of large social groups away from the perhaps as yet excessive challenge of democratic responsibility and back to dependence on authority figures, which themselves are then endowed with the attributes of parental and shadow archetypes which control the movements of the group from the depths of the unconscious. As Ernst Toller once put it, "The desire for a dictator is the desire for castration."

In considering next how the totalitarian situation may be avoided or resisted, an apparently political problem will serve to illuminate an educational one, namely that of totalitarianism in the school with its symptoms of violence and delinquency. By its nature totalitarianism only establishes itself when the political, economic and psycho-spiritual condition of society is of such a kind as either by the sins of commission or more often those of omission to invite it. This means that once established with all the equipment of modern power at its disposal, a totalitarian government cannot be resisted effectively from within by any of the traditional methods of conspiracy and that, if it is overthrown from without by alien conquest, its essential ingredients — those which originally brought it into being — are not destroyed but only and very temporarily driven underground. Resistance is beside the mark unless the instruments of that resistance themselves partake of the mystique in a complete sense of which totalitarianism is its daemonic shadow part. Dr Zimmer has expressed this truth quite clearly:

"The power of evil cannot be crushed or defeated by counter-aggression. It has to be checkmated by the mere sight of a superiority attained by self-conquest and self-sacrifice: by the mere sight of a plentitude acquired through the integration, in a recognisable form, of its own black essence. The power of evil has to be made to collapse and dissolve in despair of its own vain, purely destructive nothingness: otherwise after it has regained its strength and has stripped away the fetters of its under-world dungeon, there will be another war. Every lack of integration in the human sphere asks for its antagonistic co-operation."[25]

Beyond Totalitarianism

We would do well to meditate on what is involved in the transcending of totalitarianism both in the individual man and woman and in society collectively. If totalitarianism has its roots in the undue psychological frustration of individual and collective instinctive drives, in the economic contradictions of capitalist society and the political inadequacy of the conventionally liberal forms of representative government, then, where resistance is impossible, only transcendence remains, with the following three premises. First there must exist a sufficient number of individuals to initiate a social momentum, who have been weaned from a psychological dependence on external authority figures, whether religious or political; this implies the recognition by them of another object which they can venerate. The only valid object for many modern Westerners is the self in its Jungian sense, for as Gabriel Marcel has written:

"It can never be too strongly emphasised that the crisis which western man is undergoing today is a metaphysical one: there is probably no more dangerous illusion than that of imagining that some readjustment of social or institutional conditions could suffice of itself to appease a contemporary sense of disquiet which rises in fact from the very depth of man's being."[26]

Secondly, there must be the acceptance of the need for a world economic plan to meet population and food problems, and within this global context some kind of joint production board for social use rather than private profit. Thirdly, there must be the creation of at least a political unit to supersede the archaism of petty nationalism. These three premises presuppose a common belief in essentials about the nature of man, negatively to the extent of a repudiation of the idea that he exists to be the victim of Belsen or the executioner of Hiroshima and positively to an affirmation of the reality and indestructability of spirit, a faith such as that incomparably summarised by Wordsworth:

> Should the whole frame of earth by inward throes
> Be wrenched or fire come down from far to scorch
> Her pleasant habitations, and dry up
> Old Ocean, in his bed left singed and bare,
> Yet would the living Presence still subsist
> Victorious, and composure would endure,
> And kindlings light the morning — presage sure
> Of day returning and of life revived.[27]

In Cromwell, Napoleon, Lenin, Lincoln, Gandhi and Hitler are displayed on the horizontal of history the typical case histories of the ego on the vertical of personality. Because, as we develop, we become ego-conscious in a new way, and suffer that anguish and joy of separation, initiation and return, we can really form contact with these heroes, with a gigantic access of strength and confidence, a feeling of 'reassuring liaison' with the glorious adventures of our species. At the same time, we shall have learnt from the story of each one of these heroes the tragic truth that no human ego can escape destruction sooner or later whether at the hands of friend, foe or time. To achieve that result we must ourselves of course have perceived the limitations of the ego and realised that its sole justification lies in its transcendence of itself. One example will serve to elucidate this point: it is suggested by Lewis Mumford in his great work, *The Condition of Man.* There he depicts what has happened to European man since the Renaissance, when the ego-transcending mechanism, provided by Christian faith, became increasingly less valid for him either individually or socially. "Deprived of society, the Ego loses any confining sense of its own proper dimensions; it swims between insignificance and infinity, between the hidden sorrows of Werther and the visible triumph of Napoleon; between the desperation of suicide and the arrogance of godhead."[28]

Having realised, for example, how Napoleon was apparently a saviour to Frenchmen and a devil to Englishmen, we must strive to perceive how a study of conflict in the legendary and historical scene leads precisely to this crisis that Mumford's words suggest. It is a crisis archetypally portrayed in the legend of Orestes and admirably summarised by Gai Eaton as follows: "In truth slayer and slain are one, but upon the stage on which creation is played out, they are enemies, and the slayer has committed a sin; it is such a sin as the heroes of Greek drama commit — one that could not be avoided, and yet for which atonement is required."[29]

In brief this is the predicament of the hero who has discovered his ego and then become caught by its demands and identified with them: in psychological language the typical problem of the permanently arrested adolescent, refusing or incapable of an advance into adulthood. "Thus the legends and mythologies of the world are full of a submerged warning to man against the danger of indefinitely exceeding a part of himself at the expense of totality in personality."[30]

4

The Theme of Love in Education

"The best thing we can do for those we love
Is to help them to escape from us."

(Friedrich Von Hügel)

As in our childhood we begin to discover ourselves through the medium of our parental relationship, so as we grow older we get to know ourselves further through the medium of relationships with others of our own and the opposite sex.

Indeed it is the paradoxical essence of the matter that the ego can only become aware of itself in relationship to other egos on whom it is dependent for the very sense of its own identity — and they on it. Something of this has already been explored in terms of hero and adversary, and our enquiry must now be extended to the interdependence of boy and girl, the mutuality of lovers and the inevitable limitations of all merely egocentric partnerships.

The basic postulate from which analytical psychology starts out is that the sexual relationship is always a quartet and never a duet. Two complementaries in men and women constitute a quadruple phenomenon; this is caused by the existence physiologically and psychologically of the male within the female and the female within the male, although the woman tends to remain unconscious of her masculine nature and the man of his feminine one. The relationship between the male and female ingredients of personality is described in Jungian terms as the anima-animus mechanism. The anima is the name given to man's individually and collectively unconscious feminine side, which he can at first only see in the form of a projection on to some actual or imagined woman. The animus is the name given to woman's individu-ally and collectively unconscious masculine side, which she can at first only see in the form of a projection on to some actual or imagined man. By means of this deep and subtle device the music of the sexual quartet begins to sound, because there are always four instruments playing, a man, his anima, a woman, her animus, each pair playing at once flesh and blood people and fantasy images produced according to the needs of the respective partners. In so far as the fantasy reality and the actual reality correspond, all is well: in so far as they do not, the music is out of tune and may and generally does end in tragic discords. As will be elucidated later, the great fallacy of romantic love consists in believing that correspondence can either be fully attained or sustained if the lovers concerned are nothing but egos. It is particularly easy to realise this when it is remembered that both of these archetypes, anima and animus, are intimately connected with the 'shadow' and cannot be grasped in anything approaching entirity until the shadow has been acknowledged. That is to say, both the masculine and feminine primordial images have their negative and destructive aspects, a fact which is recognised in the phrases *"femme fatale"* and "demon lover". Each of these clearly suggests a seductive power luring consciousness away and back into the cavern of the unconscious.

Mythology, history and literature are full of examples of the complex relationships at play in the quartet of sex.[1] Examples of the anima are Rima in Hudson's *Green Mansions,* Rider Haggard's *She* or Tennyson's *Lady of the Lake.* Examples of the animus are Greatheart in *Pilgrim's Progress,* Rochester in *Jane Eyre* or the Mysterious Stranger in Ibsen's *Lady from the Sea.* What happens when there are great correspondences within the quartet with all their potentialities for positive and negative development is superbly portrayed in the great love stories of the world: three utterly different instances are Tristan and Isolde, Sir William Temple and Dorothy Osborne, Prince Albert and Queen Victoria.

It is important to understand that the anima has the further connotation of soul or muse and the animus that of intellect or reason-led spirit: thus they can be the source of the most sublimely creative of human activities and also, if abused through ignorance or deliberate malice, of untold misery and pain. To the natural question as to whether man has an animus and a woman an anima, the only possible reply will be in the first case that the more fully consciously a man realises his anima so will his conscious male functioning be improved and enriched, and to that extent the animus aspect of him be more completely operating. In the second case the answer must surely be that generally speaking woman has not had an anima because until recent times and for largely physiological reasons she herself has been too unself-conscious to be anything more than the object of man's projected anima. She can and does have an anima when, having gained and held a position of greater objective consciousness, her now fulfilled masculinity in turn operates to constellate an anima figure, be it wise old woman or any other, that then improves and enriches her own conscious, feminine functioning. It would be more correct to conceive of 'Women's Lib' in this way rather than in the form it often regrettably takes, namely that of cheap, male stridency.[2]

Cut adrift from the parental matrix, we venture out into an alien, sometimes friendly and sometimes hostile world, and it is in keeping with the laws of life that the instruments which we use in young manhood and womanhood to explore our environment are largely sexual. By this is meant no more and no less than that most social relationships to be meaningful and therefore of educational significance need to be endowed with a certain degree of perfectly legitimate, emotional, sexual interest.

At some stage of adolescence the strongest experience of the 'other' is felt in relationship to a specific other person. This culminates mostly in attachment to someone of the opposite sex, although it begins quite commonly with deep devotion to someone perhaps a year or two senior of the same sex. Expressed in less strictly psychological terms, the proposition runs as follows: every boy has a feminine side to his personality and every girl a masculine one to hers. These are the opposite and mostly unconscious counterparts in their conscious outward and visible persons. It is an essential stage in growing up to realise this correspondence and then gradually to bring the two halves into harmony with each other.

It is a strange, fascinating and exciting fact that the means whereby this occurs are curiously contradictory, although they are again part of the overall process through which human consciousness does develop. The mechanism of personality is such that an individual learns to know who he is by first seeing the as yet unconscious bits of himself projected on to and mirrored in someone or something else and then after a while withdrawing the projection he has learnt to recognise as such. The opposite sexes provide one another with suitable objects for this exercise. For every boy and girl there must be the other girl and boy in whom each can see his as yet unknown other half reflected. Not just anyone will do! He or she must be a sufficiently attractive hook for the conscious ego opposite to desire to catch hold of, but he and she are of course persons in their own rights too. It is here that trouble so often begins and where, as will be argued later, the school curriculum can be of positive assistance. For the immense jealousy and possessiveness of the ego strive to make of the hook a mere convenience. It does so either by pretending that the hook is the ego without allowing to it any individuality of its own, or it takes advantage of the hook's complementary nature to itself by permitting it to be only what the ego is not. In both cases the result is the same, namely psychological murder. In the former case it is to say, "I need you to be me — you do not exist except as part of me — I will destroy anything that dares to pretend otherwise." In the latter case it is to say, "Because I am blond, you must be brunette; because I am fat, you must be thin — you are nothing in fact but your brunetteness or your thinness." Such murder is the inevitable outcome of all attempts to base a lasting relationship between individuals on the essentially ego-centred romantic concept of love. The positive and constructive side of this quadruple relationship is best conveyed by the well-known expressions, "She brings out the best in him" or "He brings out the best in her". This means that the hook is being used as a convenience but with respect and not in such a way or in any way to injure the opposite partner's own individuality. It means that my lover is revealing me to myself, a truth which all romance from the most exalted to the most banal has always emphasised. It is the only explanation of the astonishment we all tend to feel at other people's love relationships. 'I can't think what he sees in her (or she in him)' we say, but the answer is simply and utterly satisfying when it is mutual, namely that each finds in the other those parts of himself or herself which are previously below the level of consciousness.

When to the complex nature of these hook-ego relationships are added the tremendously wide variations and possible combinations of psychological type, sensational, emotional, reasonable, intuitive, and capable of extraversion or introversion, it may seem remarkable that men and women ever do succeed in forming lasting and satisfying relationships with one another. But here they are aided by three powerful influences: one, nature's instinctual drives; two, society's conventional pressures, and three, the bliss and blessing of a mysterious third element that can enter into, sustain and hallow the relationship. All the great love stories of the world are tales of infatuation in which two lovers seek and for a time find the highest bliss in each other's arms. But notice that there are one of two turns to the romance which always occur. Either the lovers' idyll is prevented or destroyed by some alien intruding force, thus ending as the very greatest love stories like that of Romeo and Juliet do end in tragedy. Or else the idyll is transmuted into something else; the main features are then no longer the two lovers' personal passions and preoccupations but something greater than either of them.

The recorded experience of the ages does undoubtedly suggest that the individual gets to know and become what he is very largely by means of this relationship with the opposite sex. It is therefore astonishing that today when for the first time most young people in our civilisation, thanks to the findings of psychology, can attain a fair idea of the immense importance and complexity of the sexual bond, they almost entirely lack any kind of initiation into some understanding of it. They are left to shift for themselves, and the only and highly misleading impression they are given by their elders is the "sex is nothing but" one. By this is implied that, provided the young couple know all about birth control (how many do?), there is nothing more to the sexual bond than nipping in and out of bed with one another as the "urge" impels. Such an impression is strengthened by the undoubted fact that boys and girls in their teens are physically quite ready for and capable of sexual intercourse. Moreover economic and social pressures, such as provocative advertisements, incite them to immediate sexual gratification, while 'real-life' circumstances often compel them to postpone fulfilment for another eight or ten years.

No wonder the romantic view of love has received some hard knocks. The teenagers of the present generation are too shrewd and realistic to be able to deceive themselves into thinking that the traditional theory of pre- if not post- and post- if not pre-marital chastity and of Mr Right Man and Mrs Right Woman marrying and settling down to family life and children will wash any longer. Because they cannot see this aspect of human affairs as part of a larger complex they therefore assume that the sexual bond is bound to be merely one of convenience, to be cancelled whenever either or both partners get bored with it. They are of course entirely correct in drawing this conclusion as long as that sexual bond is being thought of in terms of the union between two egos only.

If the paradise pleasures and hellish sorrows are not catered for intelligently within the educational context of home and school, they will be greedily and often somewhat sordidly grabbed in the back seat plushiness of cars and cinemas. It is not less but better sex interest that must be our goal. To achieve this we must not be afraid to see it take its proper, disproportionately large, place in early life on the wise assumption that not to allow youthful affection to be passionate by artificially trying to mute or deflect it is to ensure that later adolescent and adult passion will not be affectionate. By means of the images as will now be discussed we can be introduced through our own emotional experiences of attraction and repulsion to a deeper conception of the nature of the sexual bond, one which is no longer based on the frantic and futile attempts of two egos to resolve the discords which their intimacy must cause but on the calm meeting in mutuality of two personalities, both of whom have discovered and are living from their own no longer egocentric midpoints.

Helen of Troy belongs to the cultural ancestry of most Europeans, so that her story would be a natural choice for the feminine example of the 'other' from ancient history. The manifest content of the material could be viewed in

many different ways, but it should include at some stage an
explanation of the archaeological work on the supposed site
of Troy, its location in time and place and the elucidation of
the main outline of the Graeco-Trojan struggle as it has come
down to us, together with the identification of the roles
played by Menelaeus, Paris, Hector and Achilles, Odysseus
and the Wooden Horse. When the outline of the tale has once
been firmly established in our minds, we may play with it as
we desire. There is room for every conceivable kind of
different treatment illustrated by appropriate quotations
from Marlowe's *Dr Faustus,* Giradoux's *The Trojan War Will
Not Take Place* and even Offenbach's comic opera *La Belle
Hélène.*

Let us ponder the following passage from the *Iliad* which
describes how Helen joined Priam and the elders on the walls
of Troy immediately prior to the duel between Paris and
Menelaeus:

"When they saw Helen coming to the tower, they lowered
their voices. 'Who on earth,' they asked one another, 'could
blame the Trojan and Achaean men at arms for suffering so
long for such a woman's sake? Indeed, she is the very image
of an immortal goddess. All the same, and lovely as she is, let
her sail home and not stay here to vex us and our children
after us'."[3]

How far, it might next be asked, is one woman's beauty,
however remarkable, enough to account for or justify a ten
years' war? Why is it that men in after ages have continued to
idealise Helen? The manner in which questions such as these
are debated will indicate just how much interpretation we
can profitably engage in individually or collectively. We must
be fully aware of the latent significance of the Helen figure,
why it is that "her lips have sucked forth man's soul" for
centuries. We must recognise she is ambivalent, ageless,
archetypal, a primordial image, peculiarly suited to the
carrying of a projection by a man of his anima, and that
conversely she is the eternally feminine that every woman
both longs and fears to be.

This example, together with that of the career of Mark
Antony, should help to pose vigorously the question how far
individual human entanglements, motivated by passionate

love, can, do, ought to influence history? Is the world ever well lost for love? Two images are treated, first that of the political and constitutional position as Julius Caesar reached the zenith of his power, and secondly that of the utterly different court of the Egyptian queen, away across the Mediterranean waters but already visited by Caesar at one stage of his career. Striding into these two pictures would come the figure of Mark Antony: his link with the conspirators of Caesar's death, his activities at home and abroad, the magnetism of his personal character and the fevered fascination exercised over him by Cleopatra, should all be described. Who can resist the spectacle of Antony becoming "the bellows and the fan to cool a gipsy's lust"?

The love story of Abelard and Heloise was played out on a scene most noticeably different from classical Greece and Rome because of its Christian setting. The fact that the pattern of human love was at that period seen as part of a far larger divine pattern dominates our medieval example, for we today live in an age when for the majority of men and women that particular divine pattern is no longer significant. Involved in the subject matter are doctrinal convictions, psychological attitudes and human passions. As regards the manifest content of the lesson material, emphasis will fall almost entirely on the third of these, which will in fact constitute the pedagogical scenario. Against the overall medieval background of France there can be set the simple, deeply moving, even shocking tale of the two lovers' lives and encounter. Much can be learnt from the Helen Waddell novel, particularly as illuminating the nature of the bond of human love.[4]

"Is love then lust?" asks Heloise in *Peter Abelard:* to which Gilles de Vannes replies, "Its root is lust." This little piece of dialogue provides a piece of fundamental sex education. It leads to a consideration of what is implied in the act of sexual intimacy and to an exploration of what actually constitutes reality in the meeting of two individual personalities.

Here, what is said and what is implied are obviously matters of crucial and delicate importance, and we can only hope to advance through our own deep understanding of the physical and mystical problems with which Abelard and

Heloise were struggling. The essence of these lies surely in the fact that for each partner there was a tremendous projection mechanism of anima-animus at work which was vastly complicated by the image of the Godhead in its medieval form, which they both possessed but which they found impossible to bring into harmony with their own desires. The distinction, previously alluded to, between ego and self, is clearly demonstrated in Abelard's own comment on why he was so attached to Heloise: "Because I loved you beyond measure and longed to hold you for ever." And in that quite typical utterance of egocentric romantic love we can perceive the clue to its shipwreck. The ego is of time, not of eternity; it simply cannot love for ever.

From the woman's side, as Etienne Gilson[5] so finely puts it, "From the very moment she became his wife, Heloise would never again be sure that she was not becoming an accomplice to Abelard's moral fall for the purpose of satisfying her personal interest. . . . She felt she had sinned against Abelard, not against God. The real tragedy of the action lies in the profound sincerity with which they both played the comedy of sanctity."

The truth, contained in the latent significance of the material, is of course that in each aspect of the relationship there was a third element active: psychologically the animus-anima clash, socially the rigid religious corrections of medieval society. Somehow we must learn to appreciate the deep wisdom contained in Peter the Venerable's superb comment to Heloise when writing to her about Abelard's death: "Christ is sheltering him, I say, in His bosom in your place, as a second you." Translated into humdrum modern parlance, what Peter is saying is that the enduring essence of their relationship — all that which their egos were seeking in ephemeral union and which suffered such tragic ruin — was intact, inviolate, in the Christos, the timeless, still centre of the cosmos, in the redemptive third of Buber's I-Thou relationship "What do I want out of a love relationship? What can I give to it? How enduring do I believe it can be?" The images of these lovers can help teenage and adult readers to answer those questions. They are, in fact, an instruction and initiation into the delicate intimacy of human love, and this process requires of the initiate some such understanding of human affection as is contained in the following words of Gustav Thibon:

"Intimacy is the great test of love. . . . The slow discovery of the reality of the loved being destroys little by little the inner idol of the loved one, the idol that was none other than the idealised projection of the Self, the image of what the lover himself lacked. The discovery of the other is a bitter experience for narcissistic idolatry."[6]

As has already been suggested, this bitterness can only be handled and redeemed, so that the sweetness of love is preserved, under the guardianship of what could be called the redemptive third. When two human beings really love one another, each recognises that his capacity for always loving depends on the presence of that mysterious element which Buber has described as distinguishing the I-Thou relationship from all others. It is the acknowledgement, often incoherent, inelegant and ungrammatical, by true lovers of their share in a common deep source, a mutual experience of wholeness.

5

The Theme of the Ultimates in Education

"The structure of the human being is such that a man cannot live his life or understand himself without some ultimate concern that he takes as the that-beyond-which-there-is-nothing of his world. This is indeed his god and the articulation of his life in terms of it is his religion."

(W. Herberg)[1]

If the lesson being learnt in the previous chapter is correct, namely that love between persons can only be sustained on an ego-transcended basis, than the enquiring student may legitimately enquire further concerning the nature of that basis, of what it is composed, how it may be recognised, and how its claims to obedience may be validated. Such demands used to be met by the traditional religions of East and West, but for many of us today their language has become meaningless, they no longer 'speak to our condition'. It is certainly not possible to "build a traditionally solid house on a metaphysically condemned site".[2] An effective education has to discover fresh modes of meeting what is essentially a spiritual and religious challenge, namely to define the issue that, in the words of Paul Tillich, 'concerns a man ultimately'. In 1965 Philip Leon wrote a book with the significant title, *Beyond Belief and Unbelief: Creative Nihilism*.[3] It was aimed at what he called 'the Ishmaelites or the Displaced Persons of the world of the Spirit', and these are the bulk of young people in the world today. Their best method of advance towards those ultimates being sought with such increasing appetite are along three avenues, those of art, depth psychology and some adjacent fields of science.

The Avenue of Art

In *World Cultures and World Religions*[4] Hendrick Kraemer remarked: "Art, being in our present epoch of religious and philosophical diversity and atrophy, the most universal, easily understandable language between men of culture all over the world, and so being practically the substitute religion of today, is a great winner of souls."

That is why there should be included in all curricula some study of the origins of artistic activity, its blossoming in a variety of civilisations into many different cultural canons and its manifestation in that modern art which for the first time in history is global in its inspiration and impact. In his book *Icon and Idea*[5] Sir Herbert Read argued that since the Renaissance Western man has begun to suffer from a corruption of consciousness caused by the scientific compulsion (compare the Faust story) that has tempted him to "hold on to sensation, so inevitably dissociating himself from it and becoming ultra-critical of it. The artist, that is to say, was content to give a deliberate illustration of intellectual concepts and religious dogmas that had never entered his consciousness as sensation or feelings, but were present to him as already received ideas, as lifeless formulas.[6] He explained how this process has in our own time reached a self-correcting climax:

"The post-Renaissance period should be regarded as one in which an infinite refinement of accepted symbols took place, and, as a parallel or consequent development, there was an infinite refinement of imagination and thought. But a time came when all that could be done had been done — refinement ended in sophistication, and little remained but repetition and return. But out of this weariness and fantasy a new consciousness was to be born — the consciousness of the unconscious. A further attempt was made to circumvent all ideals, whether of God or of Man, and to present not the illusion of the real but the reality of consciousness itself — subjective reality."[7]

Is it not possible to detect in that phrase, "a new consciousness came to be born", traces of an elusive new credal architecture and metaphysical base for which the search is on? Contemporary art surely does reveal a "cleavage between our mechanical and materialistic civilisation and the aesthetic and spiritual values that constitute culture".[8] It is a cleavage which the contemporary young themselves know much about in both the expression and observation of their own aesthetic impulses. How far, we may enquire, does modern art provide the creative means to give concrete significance to the new view of 'the region of that secret place whose primaeval power nurtures all evolution'?[9] How far does that 'secret place' correspond to the nature of the ego-transcended basis which we have postulated as being necessary to define? How far can a growing "consciousness of the unconscious", especially as portrayed in art, succeed in helping to remove the cleavage? The answer to this last question is, a very long way indeed. "The totality of modern art, in all its vast diversity, unfolds around a mysterious centre, which as chaos and blackness, is pregnant with a new doom, but also with a new world."[10] In order to justify such a claim as this evidence must now be examined from the field of depth psychology for the existence and role of the unconscious in general and in particular the self or "mysterious centre"; this in Jungian terms is the crossroads and core of human personality.

The Avenue to the Self

Entrance to this avenue is easier as the invisible world begins to become accessible to the experimental method.[11] Now the experience of wholeness, which includes always both sides of consciousness, super- and sub-, whether it is the artist's inspired insight or the scientist's informed guess, seems always to spring from a previous awareness of incompleteness, often vividly apprehended through suffering, such as the wound of Amfortas before the healing of Parsifal. "The religious consciousness is awakened when we encounter a network of great contradictions running through our human life. . . . We cannot regain the sense of security until we take hold of something over-riding the contradictions."[12]

It is therefore necessary to equip ourselves with psychological instruments capable of demonstrating the existence of something in ourselves that is not only our body and our ego, though both of these are essential to its discovery. It is what Jung called the 'self', the 'midpoint of the personality', and although theologically it could be regarded as the 'Inner Light' or the 'godhead immanent', it will be best to give it a neutral-toned classification, such as Factor X, thus not offending the reluctant or sceptical adventurer. It is "a superior inner authority which decides the outcome of conflicting duties or tendencies" according to Jung, who has described it clinically and fully and from whom we may take a further passage to clarify the concept still further.

"Psychology is doomed to cancel itself out as a science and therein precisely it reaches its scientific goal. Every other science has so to speak an outside; not so psychology, whose object is the inside subject of all science.

"Psychology therefore culminates of necessity in a developmental process which is peculiar to the psyche and consists in integrating the unconscious contents into consciousness. This means that the psychic human being becomes a whole, and becoming whole has remarkable effects on ego-consciousness which are extremely difficult to describe."

These 'remarkable effects', without any pathological accompaniments, are what we are after, though of course their full realisation is a task for the mature. Jung continues:

"Once these (the unconscious components of the personality) are made conscious, it results not only in their assimilation to the already existing ego-personality but to a transformation of the latter. . . . The closest analogies to an alteration of the ego are to be found in the field of psycho-pathology, where we meet not only with neurotic dissociations but also with the schizophrenic fragmentation, or even dissolution, of the ego. In this field, too, we can observe pathological attempts at integration — if such an expression be permitted. These consist in more or less violent irruptions of unconscious contents into consciousness, the ego proving itself incapable of assimilating the intruders. . .

"But if the structure of the ego-complex is strong enough to withstand their assault without having its framework fatally dislocated, then assimilation can take place. In that event there is an alteration of the ego as well as of the unconscious contents. Although it is able to preserve its structure, the ego is ousted from its central and dominating position, and thus finds itself in the role of a passive observer who lacks the power to assert his will under all circumstances, not so much because it has been weakened in any way, as because certain considerations give it pause. That is, the ego cannot help discovering that the afflux of uncon-scious contents has vitalised the personality, enriched it and created a figure that somehow dwarfs the ego in scope and intensity. This experience paralyses an over-egocentric will and convinces the ego that in spite of all difficulties it is better to be taken down a peg or two than to get involved in a hopeless struggle in which one is invariably handed the dirty end of the stick. In this way the will, as disposable energy, gradually subordinates itself to the stronger factor, namely to the new totality-figure I call the 'Self'. Naturally, in these circumstances, there is the greatest temptation simply to follow the power-instinct and to identify the ego with the 'self' outright, in order to keep up the illusion of the ego's mastery. In other cases the ego proves too weak to offer the necessary resistance to the influx of unconscious contents and is therefore assimilated by the unconscious, which produces a blurring or darkening of ego-consciousness and its identification with a pre-conscious wholeness."

But who has ever pretended that initiation into the spiritual life is not fraught with danger? Our task is both to strengthen the ego and to prepare it for eventual alliance with the 'self'. "Conscious wholeness consists in a successful union of ego and self, so that both preserve their intrinsic quali-ties."[13]

The whole process can be illustrated from Melville's tale of *Moby Dick,* which is particularly useful as showing that an essential phase in the search for wholeness is learning how to accept one's own 'shadow' side, one's inferior function (see Chapters III and VIII). In his pursuit of the white whale Captain Ahab himself becomes the image of the thing he hated.

"By physical defiance, by physical contact, Ahab cannot rout and capture Moby Dick: the odds are against him; and if his defiance is noble, his methods are ill-chosen . . . it is easier to wage war than to conquer in oneself the tendency to be partial, vindictive and unjust; it is easier to demolish one's enemy than to pit oneself against him as in intellectual combat which will disclose one's own weaknesses and provin-cialities. And that evil Ahab seeks to strike is the sum of one's enemies. He does not bow down to it and accept it:

therein lies his heroism and virtue: but he fights it with its own weapons and therein lies his madness. All the things that Ahab despises when he is about to attack the whale, the love and loyalty of Pip, the memory of his wife and child, the sextant of science, the inner sense of calm, which makes all external struggle futile, are the very things that would redeem him and make him victorious.

"Man's ultimate defence against the universe, against evil and accident and malice, is not by any fictitious resolution of these things into an absolute which justifies them and utilises them for its own ends . . . Man's defence lies within himself, not within the narrow, isolated ego, which may be overwhelmed, *but in that self which we share with our fellows* and which assures us that, whatever happens to our own carcasses and hides, good men will remain to carry on the work, to foster and protect the things we have recognised as excellent."[14]

The process of attaining conscious wholeness does not necessarily carry any theological implications. Nevertheless the self, as thus conceived, does bear unmistakably the same kinds of marks and seems to perform the same kinds of function as does what theologians call the Godhead Immanent, the Inner Light, the Atman of the Brahman, the Jewel in the Lotus. Its existence helps to explain this remark made by a young man recently: "I don't believe in God, but I respond to him."

From a quite different source there is comparable affirmation in literary terms of the psychological process by means of which archetypal energy can be transformed into conscious spirit: "For those of us who cannot accept the dogmas of any religion as uniquely revealed by God, faith may be possible that the more universal ideas or patterns underlying the doctrines are God-given, their evolution into greater clarity and relevance to life part of the Divine intention for man."[15]

This second avenue of advance gives grounds at least for belief in the possibility of consciously experiencing wholeness. So, with this and the 'mysterious centre' implied by much modern art, there are already two entities for hearts 'to cling to and confide in, Martin Luther's definition of God'.

The Avenue of Adjacent Fields of Science

Awareness of these two kinds of entity link up with certain advances in modern science, and all three offer an ultimate standpoint from which to regard the phenomenon of death. "Strictly speaking, Science does not know of death, but only of change, for science uses the word 'death' only to connote a natural process, an end to every form of life — a part of the cycle of life, to be observed in all nature. Seed, shoot, bud, flower, fruit, seed is the complex cycle: why regard any of these changes as climacteric?"[16]

Now as we have already seen (p.51) man's greatest shadow has always been what is called death. The shadow of death can only become meaningful and therefore be tolerated from the standpoint of totality, as already defined in aesthetic and psychological terms. Moreover it is this standpoint which is receiving increasing illumination from the fields of biology and parapsychology. In both of them it is the theme of emerging consciousness that commands attention:

"In the sciences the tendency to seek a logical or causally homogeneous description of natural things designed after the pattern of mathematics is on the decline. It is giving way to a trend originating in philosophy, psychology and atomic physics, to stress the bi-polar character of the phenomenal world and of time. The new trend is changing the structure of the sciences. Foreshadowed in Nicholas of Cusa's Coincidentia Oppositorum and similar conceptions in Eastern and Western philosophy, this description, though logically not homogeneous, is only apparently contradictory: it is bi-polar; that is, it expresses simultaneously two views which, though different, are both requisite to our picture of a particular object. This transformation of science, because of its archetypal character, may lead to a new correspondence between the sciences and the humanities, based on a dual (dynamic and dimensional) description of matter."[17]

It is this 'new correspondence', as it pertains to biology and parapsychology, which is one of the considerations that makes possible the entertainment of the whole ides of this book, namely the construction of a bridge across time.

A striking contribution in this field was made by Sir

Alister Hardy in the first series of his Gifford Lectures.[18] In them he advocates "a theism which is derived empirically from the study of nature, man and human history." (p.11) "Has modern biology destroyed the basis for a theistic religion?" he asks, and he answers his own question: "I do not mean a belief in a deity with an anthropomorphic image. I do, however, at least mean a belief in an 'extra-sensory' contact with a Divine Power which is greater than and in part lies beyond the individual self."[19] Later, as we shall see, he qualifies this statement regarding divine power, thus, I believe, making his viewpoint more widely acceptable than if he stuck rigidly to this notion. As regards 'extra-sensory contact', the following measured judgement of Professor H. H. Price is worth pondering:

"Telepathy is something which ought not to happen at all, if the Materialist Theory were true. But it does happen. So there must be something seriously wrong with the Materialistic Theory, however numerous and imposing the normal facts which support it may be. . . . If they (the queer facts of psychical research) show, as I think they do, that the Materialistic conception of human personality is untenable, and if they throw a new light on the age-old conflict between the scientific and religious outlooks, we shall have to conclude that Psychical Research is one of the most important branches of investigation which the human mind has ever undertaken."[20]

The really compelling reflection on this matter is to be found in Sir Ronald Fisher's Eddington Memorial Lecture, 'Creative Aspects of Natural Law':

"The surface or limit separating the inner from the outer life of each living thing is also, in our experience, the true seat of our consciousness, the boundary of the objective and the subjective, where we experience, through our imperfect sense-organs, what comes to us from outside and, with at least equal obscurity, that which rises into consciousness from within. If consciousness is, as it would seem, the symbol, or even the means, of unification in each being, this is the region to which creative activity could most fitly be traced."

"It is in this field (that of experiments in telepathy),"
continues Sir Alister Hardy, "that I believe science will come
to make its second great contribution to natural theology by
showing the reality of part of the Universe outside the world
of the physical senses. It is in this apparently non-material
part of the world that the power we call God must lie: some
source of influences to which Man can have access in an
extra-sensory way by the communicative act we call
prayer."[21] "I believe that the living world is as closely linked
with theology as it is with physics and chemistry: that the
Divine element is part of the natural process — not strictly
supernatural but paraphysical."[22] "At the very least I expect
this power of which we speak may be some subconscious
shared reservoir of spiritual 'know how' which we call Divine
(perhaps something like the 'species mind') that I have
suggested; I think, however, it is far more likely that above
this there is something much more wonderful to which we
give the name. God. *But even if it should be shown, and I do
not believe it will, that this whole conception is a purely
psychological one and, if, in some way, this mind-factor
should eventually be proved to be entirely of physico-
chemical origin — it would not to my mind destroy the joy or
help of the experience we may still call Divine any more than
it would destroy the glorious beauty felt in poetry or art.*"[23]

The 'region of creative activity' referred to by Sir Ronald
Fisher corresponds to the other two entities previously
mentioned. It is therefore along these three avenues that the
theme of the ultimates may be fruitfully explored; some
aspects of their historical dimensions form the subject of the
second half of this book.

Part two

HISTORY

6

The Advent of the Psycho-Historian

"The true philosophy of history consists in the insight that in all these endless changes and their confusion we have always before us only the same, even, unchanging nature, which today acts in the same way as yesterday and always; thus it ought to recognize the identical in all events, of ancient as of modern times, of the East as of the West; and, in spite of all difference of the special circumstances, of the costumes and customs, to see everywhere the same humanity."

(Arthur Schopenhauer, *The World as Will and Idea*)[1]

All interpretations of the past which have endured, from that of Thucydides to that of Ranke, possess the quality of deep psychological insight. However, it is only in recent years that the discoveries of depth psychology have become available for application by historians and teachers of history to their respective functions. In this Chapter I shall discuss some of the uses to which these findings have begun to be put, exploring in particular the proposition that in order to make sense of any historical event, it is essential to probe it with the needle of psychological analysis.

The Psycho-Historical Dimension

The psycho-historian, not disdaining a working partnership with the bio-sociologist (see George Steiner's *In Bluebeard's Castle*[2]), proceeds on one basic hypothesis, namely that there is a significant correspondence between man's unconscious and his past (see Chapter I). This leads on to the concept of history as the record of the growth of human consciousness both individually and collectively. This is a growth from "unconscious to conscious anonymity".[3] It is a growth from "the impersonal via the personal to the transpersonal" dimension of consciousness.[4] It is the growth from what Lévy-Bruhl called *'participation mystique'* via the hero who dares to be different to the communion of saints or, in secular language, the absolute value system of men of good will. This is a process which occurs sequentially in 'profane time' but declares itself through revelation in 'sacred time'.[5] It is T. S. Eliot's "Time past and time future", pointing "to one end, which is always present". (See his poem 'Burnt Norton'.)

History may therefore be regarded as a study of the psycho-temporal process in which the individual and collective psychologies of any given epoch are correlated with its outer political and cultural attributes. For "the real continuity of history does not consist in the external forms of a civilisation, nor in the surface flow of events, but rather in the forces that are psychologically active in the depths of people."[6] Burckhardt himself remarked in *Forces and Freedom: An Interpretation of History:*[7] "The dynamics of man's life, his beliefs and his passions, comprise the material for the life and death of societies." Conversely Jung notes in his *Civilisation in Transition:*[8] "It is the cultural context which provides perspective for an understanding of the structure of human personality."

The psycho-historical dimension thus opened up by twentieth-century Western, empirical and scientific research receives curious confirmation from the traditional Eastern wisdom of Vedanta. This may be conveniently illustrated by the following passage in Erwin Schrödinger's book *My View of the World.*[9] In it he is addressing a hypothetical reader seated gazing at a mountain landscape:

"According to our usual way of looking at it, everything that you are seeing has, apart from small changes, been there for thousands of years before you. After a while — not long — you will no longer exist, and the woods and the rocks and sky will continue unchanged for thousands of years after you. What is it that has called you so suddenly out of nothingness to enjoy for a brief while a spectacle which remains quite indifferent to you? The conditions of your existence are almost as old as the rocks. . . . A hundred years ago perhaps another man sat on this spot; like you he gazed with awe and yearning in his heart at the dying light on the glaciers. Like you he was begotten of man and born of woman. He felt pain and brief joy as you do. *Was* he someone else? Was it not you yourself? What is this Self of yours? What was the necessary condition for making the thing conceived this time into you? Just you, and not someone else? What clearly intelligible, scientific meaning can this 'someone else' really have? If she, who is now your mother, had cohabited with someone else and had a son by him, and your father had done likewise, would you have come to be? Or were you living in them, and in your father's father — thousands of years ago? And even if this is so, why are you not your brother? Why is your brother not you? Why are you not one of your distant cousins? What justifies you in obstinately discovering this difference — the difference between you and someone else — when objectively what is there is the same?

"Looking and thinking in that manner you may suddenly come to see the profound rightness of the basic conviction in Vedanta: it is not possible that this unity of knowledge, feeling and choice which you call your own should have sprung into being from nothingness at a given moment not so long ago; rather, this knowledge, feeling and choice are essentially eternal and unchangeable and numerically one in all men, nay in all sensitive beings.

"But not in *this* sense — that *you* are a part, a piece of an eternal, infinite being, an aspect or modification of it, as in Spinoza's pantheism. For we should then have the same baffling question: which part, which aspect are *you?* What, objectively, differentiates it from the others?

"No, but inconceivable as it seems to ordinary reason, you — and all other conscious beings as such are all in all. Hence this life of yours which you are living is not merely a piece of the entire existence, but is in a certain sense the whole: only this whole is not so constituted that it can be surveyed in one single glance."

From the point of view of this essay there are two key phrases in that passage: one concerns the identity of the individual, the *you,* no longer to be regarded as a part of a whole but as "all in all", "in a certain sense the whole"; the second is "this whole, not so constituted that it can be surveyed in a single glance", but history has to focus it, the historian has to hold it in a steady gaze. That is the precise task of the psycho-historian, to identify and depict in the phenomena of the past that "cosmic point" where "spirit and nature meet".[10] It is his honour and privilege to reach out and clasp and then record that being in time which lies behind the becoming of time.

The Psycho-Historian at Work

In the first chapter of his splendid biography of Henry VIII[11] Professor Scarisbrick writes of him: "He was highly strung and unstable; hypochondriac and possessed of a strong streak of cruelty. Possibly he had an Oedipus complex: and possibly from this derived a desire for, yet horror of, incest, which may have shaped some of his sexual life." The reference given for this cautious but fruitful supposition — fruitful because of the illumination it gives to a piece of Tudor history — is Flugel's 'On the Character and Married Life of Henry VIII', which appears in *Psychoanalysis and History*.[12] This venture into psycho-history may now be set against the background of one of the pioneer works in this field, Norman Brown's *Life Against Death, the Psycho-analytical Meaning of History*.[13] His central thesis is well expressed in the following passage from that work: "the pattern of history exhibits a dialectic, not hitherto recognised by the historians, the dialectic of neurosis." (p.12) By this last phrase is meant the tension set up both in the individual and the collective between the impulse towards separation from origins, growth and development into self-conscious independence and the backward, regressive grasp of instinctual, devouring-mother, unconscious life: the dialectic involves a more or less tolerable degree of neurosis; when intolerable, the individual or society regresses into an earlier stage of primitivity. Here surely we hold in our hands a precious clue to an understanding of the so-called decadent periods of history. Norman Brown elaborates this notion of the growth into consciousness:

"Psycho-analytical consciousness, as a higher stage in the general consciousness of mankind, may be likewise the fulfilment of the historical consciousness, that ever-widening and deepening search for origins, which has obsessed Western thought since the Renaissance. If historical consciousness is finally transformed into psycho-analytical consciousness, the grip of the dead hand of the past on life in the present would be loosened, and man would be ready to live instead of making history, to enjoy instead of paying back old scores and debts, and to enter that state of Being which was the goal of his becoming." (p.19).

It is interesting to note the similarity between this concept of 'living' instead of 'making' history with Julian Huxley's and Teilhard de Chardin's concept of modern man's need to take conscious control of his further evolution as a species. The passage is also suggestive as providing an answer to that frequently canvassed question: what is the use of history?

We may next turn our attention to the work in the U S A of the Group for the Study of Psycho-Historical Process, which studies the "motivations behind and the relationships between seemingly unfathomable and disjointed events". More specifically there are the writings of Professor Robert Jay Lifton, who holds the Chair for Research in Psychology at Yale University and who has interested himself in the relationship between individual psychology and historical change. In his book *Thought Reform and the Psychology of Totalism: A Study of Brainwashing in China and Revolutionary Immortality*,[14] Lifton has identified what he calls "modes of symbolic immortality as the individual's inner perception of his involvement in what he calls the historical process".

Again it is of interest to lay alongside this assessment of an historical phenomenon the remarks of a psychologist and a playwright. Otto Rank spoke once of every individual's need for 'assurance of eternal survival for his Self', while Ionesco comments: "As long as we are not assured of immortality, we shall never be fulfilled, we shall go on hating each other in spite of our need for mutual love." That is why we have to learn history, to gain assurance of immortality and so the capacity to love, for, as Freud himself taught, "In the end we must begin to love in order not to fall sick."

Much of the work of Erik Erikson is an exploration of "the history of humanity as a gigantic metabolism of individual life-cycles" in which he investigates "the relationship between ego-qualities, social institutions and historical eras".

He warns us that, "There is no time left in which to be as naive historically as, in all past history, the historians have been psychologically."[15] He practises what he preaches in *Young Man Luther: A Study in Psycho-Analysis and History* (1959), *Insight and Responsibility* (1966) and *Youth and Crisis* (1969). A passage in that last book deserves quotation here because it pinpoints one of the key potential strengths of the psycho-historian:

"Past history survives in the ideal and evil prototypes, which guide the parental imagery and which colour fairy-tale and family lore, superstition and gossip and the simple lessons of early training. Historians on the whole make little use of this: they account only for the context of autonomous historical ideas and are unconcerned with the fact that these ideas reach down into the lives of generations and re-emerge through the daily awakening and training of historical consciousness in young individuals." (p.25)

In the same book (p.260) Erikson makes a passionate plea for "historical reality at last ethically cared for". Is not this the ethical spinal column so sadly lacking in most history teaching?

However it is in his latest work, *Gandhi's Truth*,[16] that Erikson has defined most clearly his concept of the role of the psycho-historian:

"If history is a collection of events which come to life for us because of what some actors did, some recorders recorded and some reviewers decided to re-tell, a clinician attempting to interpret an historical event must first of all get the facts straight. But he must apply to this task what he has learned, namely to see in all factuality some relativities which arise from the actors', the recorders' and the reviewers' motivations . . . the psycho-historian will want to enquire in some detail after the stage of life in which the actor acted, the recorder recorded and the reviewer reviewed. He will want to learn about the place of that stage in the Life-cycles of each of these individuals; and he will want to relate their life-cycles to the history of their communities." (p.55)

Two further examples of psycho-history will suffice to give the flavour of this branch of investigation: Jack Kovel's

White Racism, a Psycho-History[17] and Lucille Iremonger's *The Fiery Chariot: a Study of British Prime Ministers and the Search for Love.*[18] Kovel points out that "human instinctual conflict when projected on to culture is one of the crucial determinants of historical power" (p.8) and adds, "The power that invests history with so much dynamism is as much the product of the way people conceive of themselves, others and the world, as it is the product of machines." (p.9) Iremonger analyses in her book the Phaeton complex, so called after the Greek myth of the driver across the heavens who crashed to ruin, a psychoanalytic label given to 'emotional deprivation in childhood' which a surprisingly high percentage of British politicians who became Prime Ministers in the nineteenth and twentieth centuries had suffered. My own tentative exercises in the field of psycho-history may be inspected in *Education for World Understanding, an Appendix on Thomas More and Thomas Cromwell.*[19] In an article in *Encounter* (June 1971) Goronwy Rees explored the idea of the novel as an aid to the historian under the heading, 'Between Hope and Nihilism: Chiaromonte's Paradox of History'. (See also Chapter VII of this book for a treatment of the novel as an aid to the historian.) He describes how Chiaromonte treated the novelists, Stendhal, Tolstoy, Pasternak and others: "the novelist depicts history as seen from the inside, from within the skin of the orange. . . . In every important work of fiction," continues Chiaromonte, "we find implicit or ex-plicit, well amalgamated with the narrative or clumsily appended to it, a definite structure of ideas. There is no modern novel of any scope that does not imply a certain view of society, of history, of the world. 'It is not sufficient to be a man, one must be a system,' said Balzac." To this we might add: it is not sufficient to be a historian, one must be a system. The most obvious exponent of all is of course Marcel Proust (1871-1922). The final volume of his masterpiece carries the title of which historians might be proud, *Time Regained,* but it is in his *By Way of Sainte-Beuve* that Proust speaks most directly to our purpose:

"What intellect restores to us under the name of the past is not the past. In reality, as soon as each hour of one's life has died, it embodies itself in some material object, as do the souls of the dead in certain folk-stories, and hides there. There it remains captive, captive for ever, unless we should happen on the object, recognise what lies within, call it by its name and so set it free." (p.17)

Those last few words summarise admirably the task of the psycho-historian, "to happen on the object, recognise what lies within and so set it free", thus redeeming the past instead of becoming its slave. Perhaps some budding psycho-historian may care to apply his techniques to the roles of Parnell and Kitty O'Shea in the story of the struggle for Irish independence. Making use of Jung's psychological types, Erikson's concept of the dominant factor of the relationship to the father in determining the style of a life-cycle, and finally, a poem by Yeats, it should be possible to make sense of Michael Davitt's description of his chief, Parnell, as a cold-blooded sensualist. The fatal attraction of polarities between Parnell and Kitty O'Shea could be seen as arising from his superior functions of reason and instinct seeking and finding their complementarity in her superior functions of feeling and intuition. The temporary fusion of these two could account for the power with which Parnell pursued his mission and also the destructive element in it (the opposite inferior functions in each) which shipwrecked him.

In 'Parnell's Funeral' Yeats by means of his poetic imagination succeeds in linking the individual to the collective phenomena of this piece of history and in demonstrating the working of the past within the present.

> An age is the reversal of an age:
> When strangers murdered Emmet, Fitzgerald, Tone,
> We lived like men that watch a painted stage.
> What matter for the scene, the scene once gone:
> It had not touched our lives. But popular rage,
> Hysterica passio, dragged this quarry down.
> None shared our guilt; nor did we play a part
> Upon a painted stage when we devoured his heart.
> Come, fix upon me that accusing eye. . .
>
> Had de Valera eaten Parnell's heart,
> No loose-lipped demagogue had won the day,
> No civil rancour torn the land apart.

Had Cosgrave eaten Parnell's heart, the land's
Imagination had been satisfied,
Or lacking that, government in such hands,
O'Higgins its sole statesman had not died.

Had ever O'Duffy — but I name no more —
Their school a crowd, his master solitude;
Through Jonathan Swift's dark groves he passed, and there
Plucked bitter wisdom that enriched his blood.

"An age is the reversal of an age": contemporary contenders on the Irish stage of Eire and Ulster, as well as students of their history, require to 'eat Parnell's heart' if they are to pluck 'bitter wisdom' and so enrich their own blood today.

Is history then a thing of the past? The advent of the psycho-historian makes it possible to answer this question with a firm, paradoxical, Yes and No. It is a thing of the past because it deals with an unique dimension of human experience, that of vanishing chronological sequence. It is not a thing of the past because it is present in our contemporary lives, corresponding to the unconscious. In other words, history is a thing of the past because it is not past. The psycho-historian is our latest helper in discovering and holding on to this truth, without the acceptance of which we remain helpless, imprisoned victims of time, lodged in a Sartrean dungeon. This is a predicament well described by Professor Plumb in *Encounter* (June 1971) as "literally thousands of historians scurrying like ants over the debris of time but often possessing no more than an ant's vision". In the same article Plumb sketches the true alternative function of history: "The power of history, its position of authority within an intellectual system has, however, always derived from its capacity to explain the present and, perhaps, to indicate the future — two roles which, at present, professional history singularly fails to play."

With the aid of the psycho-historian we can begin to correct this lamentable failing, so becoming once again history's beloved because loving inheritors.

7

Fiction as 'The Third Dimension of History'

"Fancy with fact is one fact the more."
(Browning, 'The Ring and the Book')

Fiction, as E. M. Forster pointed out in *Aspects of the Novel,*[1] 'occupies that spongy tract of land which lies between poetry and history'. It is, says Gabriel Marcel in 'The Mystery of Being' (Gifford Lectures, 1952) 'through the novelist's power of creation that we can get our best glimpse of what lies behind the reverbatory power of facts'. 'Thus life would speak, if life could speak,' said Du Bois of Tolstoy's *War and Peace.* The actual title of this chapter is suggested by the definition of fiction in *The Glass Bead Game* by Hermann Hesse. I am not concerned here with the historical novel as the fictionalised behaviour of actual historical characters. It is not the re-animated characters but the created ones which interest me, that is to say, the products of the novelist's imagination in the form of a group of characters at play on a stage already set by the bare chronicled past, 'the spongy tract of land' on which may be discovered for any particular period of the past 'what lies behind the reverbatory power of facts'. Through this type of novel there may be identified the very essence of history, which surely consists of men and women being both the prisoners of their time and at the same time capable of transcending it if they so desire. Novelists, who possess a deeply perceptive genius for creation, are masters in abundance of this quality: the characters they have created constitute their author's own immortalities — Tolstoy's Pierre and Thomas Mann's Adrian Leverkühn are masterpieces of art, they are in Rilke's words 'eternity protruding into time'; they are the means whereby we may contact and recognise the timeless within the timebound, revelation within sequence, life within death.

As an introduction to the kind of technique of historical interpretation, which I shall now be attempting with two Austrian novels of the twentieth century and an American one of the nineteenth, it may be helpful to cite the novels of Patrick White.

Although Australian by birth, Patrick White grew up in England, and was educated at Cheltenham and Cambridge. After one brief return to the land of his birth and a short experience as a 'Jaqueroo' in the Australian outback, he returned to this country and then served as an Intelligence Officer in the R A F during the Second World War. After it he settled permanently in Sydney, Australia. In his few plays and in his novels White explores three themes persistently: one, the colonisation of Australia and what that has meant for successive generations of Australians; two, rather more obliquely, the ideological tensions of the world since the mid-thirties, and three, mysticism with a strong lead into it from the findings of modern depth psychology.

In *The Aunt's Story* (1948) Patrick White offers us some glimpses of the pre-1914 world in Australia and establishes one of his recurrent woman types, in this case Theodora Goodman, half mad, half wise, fey, inconsequent, who acts as a kind of crystal in which other people's characters are reflected. As one of them says of her, 'If she is not careful she will miss the bus.' And in one sense this is precisely what she does: she fails to get married, she fails to come to terms with the — for her — overseas world of Europe, and at the close of the book she is on her way to a mental institution. Yet she has not really missed the bus, and nor do we as we share her insights, particularly into what the author calls the *'Jardin Exotique'* of European drop-outs or refugee casualties living drab lives on the Riviera in the thirties. 'Surely by this time,' says one of them, 'you must understand we have entered the age of Ersatz.' Here is a direct historical allusion: that the 'have-not' countries of Europe had to make do with substitutes for the real thing in many fields of existence and how the word 'ersatz' itself came to express the counterfeit living of the post-Christian age, the world of Eliot's 'Hollow Men'. Because Theodora herself is so genuine, so completely the antithesis of ersatz, she cannot accept the decadently ersatz nature of either her Australian or European world. One of White's characters is described as having a face which 'absorbed news while remaining superior to events'. Here in one telling phrase is the clue to an understanding of that 'onlooker' consciousness of so many 'decent chaps', 'men of good will', men without qualities perhaps, who stood aside while their societies headed via the Abyssinian war and the Spanish Civil war and Munich for the cataclysm of 1939. In Chapter XII Theodora meets the mysterious stranger or wise old man, Dr Holstius, a figure incredibly analogous to that of Dr Lindner in Musil's novel, *The Man without Qualities.* Her own predicament as the one who is rejected by existing society and who is too weak or too premature to create a better one is pinpointed by a quotation from Olive Schreiner: 'When your life is most real, to me you are mad.'

In *The Tree of Man* (1956) and *Voss* (1957) White gives us the feel of Australia in the process of settlement: the former is set in 1900, a veritable 'Australian Book of Genesis'. Then in 1961 came *Riders in the Chariot,*[2] in which White is again occupied with three motifs of our times. First, the role of redemptive instinct and the harking back to primitivity in the person of the half-caste, Abo, himself a forerunner of the figure of the artist, which is to be explored in grand detail in *The Vivisector* (1970). Then secondly, there is the mad-wise woman again in the person of Miss Hare: 'Eventually I shall discover what is at the centre, if enough of me is peeled away.' Her remark is that of a person on the road to self-conscious individuation in an Australian setting. In the same book there is a masterly flashback to the plight of Jewry in Nazi Germany and Himmelfarb as a victim of anti-Semitism. There is an unuttered but discernible implication that there is much in the Australian way of life, which could, if put under pressure, produce many of the same symptoms on that continent as appeared in Europe in the thirties. The attempted crucifixion of Himmelfarb by his workmates suggests with uncanny, horrifying force the appalling likelihood that the totalitarian virus is endemic in our modern world situation.

The collection of White's short stories, *The Burnt Ones* (1964), treats of those whom the fires of the *Cities of the Plain* threaten to consume. *The Solid Mandala* (1966) explores through two brothers, Waldo and Arthur, how in the search for wholeness, evil itself and lunacy have somehow got to be accommodated. With the help of this title White manages to bestride the world of East and West: the mandala as symbol of man's struggle towards completion as an alternative to his foolhardy and fatal pursuit of perfection.

In *The Vivisector* (1970) White seems to attain full stature and to establish his strange, almost mystical link with the Austrian, Musil. Hurtle Duffield, the artist, may fittingly be compared with Adrian Leverkühn in Thomas Mann's *Dr Faustus:* he is pursuing integration through painting as Adrian does through music. Like Ulrich with Agathe, in *The Man without Qualities* (see below), he has a highly significant relationship with his sister, the hunchback Rhoda. The text of this book, which might be described as a sermon in an aesthetic key, is contained in the slogan Duffield has daubed on the wall of his privy:

> 'God the Vivisector,
> God the artist
> God . . .'

In those terse words White propounds the contemporary human predicament, which is explored at so much greater length in Musil's three volumes, namely, that if there is no God, can man, the artist, preserve himself from the destructive energy of his instinctual life? The question is posed and partially answered in the context of our age of concentration camps, Hiroshima and escalating social violence. It is as if White were saying to his readers: 'Look into the life of Hurtle Duffield, examine his pictures and then ask yourselves whether they do not indeed illuminate the fantastic excessess of a Belsen and account for the way in which ordinary men can behave as devils if they lack containers for the dark side of their unconscious lives.'

In this work, White seems to be sensing the possible direction of redemption, a theme into which he probes with almost compulsive energy in his most recent novel, *The Eye of the Storm* (1973). His characters symbolise 'modern man in search of a soul'. Because these novels have reference to so many quarters of the globe and because that search is what twentieth-century history is largely about, they can illuminate with imaginative brilliance our study of contemporary history.

Between 1914 and 1945 Austria lived through four clearly discernible phases, the collapse of the Austro-Hungarian Empire at the end of the First World War, the period of parliamentary democracy, 1919-34, the Austrian corporate state, 1934-38, assimilation to the Third Reich and defeat in the Second World War, 1938-45. Many historians have traced the course of these events and offered explanations of why and how they happened. Sometimes this has been in terms of politics and nationalities, sometimes in terms of religion, that is, Roman Catholicism versus secularism, perhaps most frequently and very convincingly in terms of economics: the 1920s' inflation and the devastating effect of the post-Versailles policies of Austria's great power neighbours. Yet all of these leave the curious observer of the human scene with a number of deep, unanswered questions.

Let us try and enter what Karl Kraus, Editor of *Die Fackel* 1911-36, called that 'research laboratory for world destruction', referring to these years. "My business," he said, "is to pin down the Age between quotation marks." Our purpose here is to probe the age with the instruments of two remarkable pieces of Austrian fiction. The kinds of questions which they may help us to answer are these. Who were the people who felt the economic shoe pinching most acutely? How strong a force really was political separatism? What impact did Freud and depth psychology have on social life and morals? Which were the constants and which the variables in Austrian national life?

"Into this country (post-1918 Austria) of barely seven million inhabitants, with its borders wide open, the remnants of the army streamed back; officers from garrisons in Hungary and Croatia, civil servants from Cracow and Ljubliana, engineers from the shipyards in Pola and Trieste, businessmen from Belgrade and the ports of the Adriatic, teachers and doctors from the Ukraine and the Carpathians, professors of the German University in Prague, mining engineers from the coal-mines in Upper Silesia, the staffs of the governors, administrators of the vast forest domains, judges, diplomats, ambassadors, builders, foremen, railwaymen — all of these streamed back into the mutilated torso of what only four years earlier had been a flourishing empire."[3]

Born in 1880, Robert Musil came of Austro-Czech parents, educated and well-to-do. As a boy he attended the notorious military academy of Weisskirchen, but, unlike the young Rilke who had suffered under its harshness a few years earlier, Musil seems to have passed through the experience unscathed though not uninfluenced. He took a university training in civil engineering, served as an Austrian officer in the First World War and from 1919 to 1921 was a civil servant. His first short novel, *Young Törless,* had been published in 1906; a few short stories and one or two plays followed. Volume I of *The Man Without Qualities* appeared in 1930, Volume II in 1932, while Volume III was still being worked on at the time of his death.[4] In 1935 a group of friends formed the Musil-Gesellshaft, on the financial support of which he relied almost entirely. In 1938, because of the Nazi take-over in Austria, he emigrated to Switzerland where he died in 1942. Although there are other publications, most of them still untranslated into English, it is in *The Man Without Qualities* that Musil's genius shines most brightly: it is here that we find illumination and explanation of what was happening to Western civilisation before 1914 and also of many of the consequences stemming from the Great War. Henry James, writing soon after the outbreak of those hostilities, remarked: 'To have to take it all now for what the treacherous years were all the while really making for and meaning is too tragic for any words.' Musil's story helps us to penetrate into the meaning of those 'treacherous years', and as a story it is often as entertaining as it is pathetic.

What is it all about? It concerns the experiences of an educated Viennese gentleman of independent means as he is drawn into a scheme, the 'Collateral Campaign' of the Imperial Habsburg Court, to celebrate the seventieth anniversary of the reign of the old Emperor, Franz Joseph, and in so doing to neutralise, if possible, the rising pretensions of its younger neighbour, the Germany of Kaiser Wilhelm II. A series of more or less intimate relations with a circle of friends culminates in Ulrich's ('the man without qualities') incestuous love of his sister, Agathe. Page after page one has the impression of a succession of falling bastions, political, economic, cultural, falling and being captured by the 'daremen' of totalitarianism or the dark instinctive forces of the unconscious symbolised by the criminal, Moosbrugger; contrasting with these is the world of big business personified by the German, Arnheim. Musil started to write *The Man Without Qualities* in the twenties and continued to work at it during the thirties, and provides a running commentary on his times by means of a fictional focus some twenty years earlier, that is, Vienna in 1913. Striking evidence of the way in which the genius of the novelist can penetrate the mystery of time past, while the historian is still struggling with the problem of mere sequence, is afforded by the following few extracts.

Musil brings us straight to the heart of our modern predicament through the mouth of his main character: "One can't be angry with one's own time without damage to oneself, Ulrich felt. And indeed he was always ready to love all those manifestations of life. What he could never manage, however, was to love them unreservedly, as is required for a general sense of well-being."[5]

Whether it is the First World War, the period 'entre deux guerres' or the Second World War, it is with a throb of recognition that one reacts to those words, 'being angry with one's own times'. Whether one fought or abstained from fighting in the two major conflicts, became a pacifist or fought in the Spanish Civil War, one's answer did 'do damage to oneself' however hard one tried to 'love all the manifestations of life unreservedly': one just did not possess enough integrity to do so. Perhaps only the saint can really affirm that everything that is, is right, and Ulrich was no saint, though we are told that he was seeking the path of saintliness.

Ulrich probes further into the contemporary malaise:

"There has arisen a world of qualities without a man to them, of experiences without anyone to experience them, and it almost looks as though under ideal conditions man would no longer experience anything at all privately, and the comforting weight of personal responsibility would dissolve into a system of formulae for potential meanings. It is probable that the dissolution of the anthropocentric attitude (an attitude that, after so long seeing man as the centre of the universe, has been dissolving for some centuries now) has finally begun to affect the personality itself; for the belief that the most important thing about experience is the experiencing of it, and about deeds the doing of them, is beginning to strike most people as naive." (p.175)

'Experiences have made themselves independent of men', 'a world of qualities without a man to them': what an incredibly neat and just parody of the men of good will of the first half of the twentieth century, how naive to believe in the effectiveness of mere experience! In his *Journals* Kierkegaard remarked, "Experience, it is said, makes a man wise. That is very silly talk. If there was nothing beyond experience it would simply drive him mad."

In his study of Arnheim, 'the superman of letters', Musil offers an extremely probing examination of what lies behind the façade of business dealings — 'the combination of commerce and idealism':

"Just as the prince of the intellect had his place in the age of princes, so the superman of letters has his place in the age of the Super-dreadnought and the Super-store. He is a particular manifestation of the mind's association with things of super-size." (p.154)

"But nowadays there are no longer any great thoughts that are accepted without question, for this sceptical age believes neither in God nor in Mankind, neither in crowns or in morality; or it believes in the whole lot of it all rolled into one, which amounts to the same thing. So businessmen, who think they cannot get along without some sort of greatness for a compass, have had to make use of the democratic dodge of replacing the immeasurable influence of greatness by the measurable greatness of influence; only this means that in the last resort whatever is clamourously advertised as great also becomes great. And it is not everyone's luck to be able to swallow this innermost core of our time without difficulty." (p.249) Indeed, does modern man believe in God or in the head of the world concern?

"After all a man conscious of his responsibilities, Arnheim told himself with conviction, even when he gives of his soul, must expend only the interest, never the capital." (p.257)

Through the character of Arnheim we come to a deeper understanding, not only of Rathenau, but Krupps, ICI, Charles Clore and Onassis, and realise why what Eric Gill said must be true throughout the contemporary context, namely that 'the business man's criterion of good is profit — the measurable greatness of influence'. The story of the last thirty years answers Musil's question unmistakably: modern man believes 'in the head of the world concern' which is each nation's GNP.

Perhaps it is in the following long meditation of Count Leinsdorf that this great novel achieves its highest measure of historical interpretation:

"There are certain family feelings that are particularly intense, and one of them was the dislike of Germany that prevailed generally in the European family of nations before 1914. Perhaps Germany was the intellectually and spiritually least unified country, and hence a country that offered everyone something to suit his own dislikes; it was the country whose old-time culture had been the first to fall under the wheels of the new era and be sliced up into high-flown phrases for the catchpenny purposes of commercialism; it was, further more, aggressive, grasping, boastful and dangerously lacking, like every excited crowd, in responsibility for its actions. But all this was, after all, only European, and it should not have been anything but, at most, a little too European for all the other Europeans. What it comes to is simply that there must be entities, what one might call displeasure images, to which disgust and disharmony cling, as it were the residue of a smouldering fire such as life nowadays leaves behind. Out of the potentiality, the It-May-Be, suddenly, to the boundless amazement of all concerned, the actual thing, the It-Is arises, and whatever chips off during this disorderly process, whatever does not fit, whatever is superfluous and does not satisfy the mind, seems to form that hatred, suspended in the atmosphere and setting up tremors among all living creatures, which is so characteristic of present-day civilisation, and which replaces a lost contentment with one's own doing by an easily obtainable discontent with the doings of others. The attempt to concentrate this displeasure on specific entities is merely part of something that is part of the oldest psychotechnical apparatus mankind possesses. So it was that the magician drew forth the carefully prepared fetish from the sick man's body, and so it is that the good Christian projects his defects into the good Jew, asserting that it is he who has lured him into publicity stunts, usury, journalism, and the like. In the course of the ages people have blamed thunder, witches, the socialists, the intellectuals and the generals, and in the last years before the war, for special reasons that are of no account whatever in comparison with the importance of the principle itself, one of the most magnificent and popular means of satisfying this queer need was Prussian Germany. For the world has lost not only God but the Devil as well. Just as it projects the Good into pleasure images, wishful fantasies, day-dreams, which it reveres for doing what one finds it impossible to do in one's person. One lets other people exert themselves while one sits there comfortably looking on: that is sport. One lets other people talk the most wildly one-sided extravagances: that is idealism. One shakes off the Evil, and what gets splashed with it is images of one's displeasure. So everything gets its place in the world and fits into some hierarchy. But this technique of hagiolatry and fattening up of scape-goats by means of projections into the outer world is not without its dangers, for it fills the world with tensions of all inner conflicts that have not been fought out. Men slaughter each other or fraternise with each other, never rightly knowing whether they are doing it quite seriously, because after all one part of oneself is outside oneself and all that happens seems to go on half in front of reality, or half behind it, as a sort of sword-play in a mirror, a sham fight of hate and love. The ancient belief in demons, which held heavenly or hellish spirits responsible for all the good and evil that came one's way in life, worked much better, more accurately and neatly, and one can only hope that as developments in psychotechnics progress we shall get back to it again." (pp.258-9)

Here Musil is playing on all the stops of historical inter- pretation by sounding out the complementarity of good and evil for all ego-centred human creatures, imprisoned in and never being in time for anything: Britain's failure, for instance, to rearm sufficiently in time in the thirties, with at the same time intimations of the need for transcendence of the good-evil dilemma. It is fascinating to pick up the various resonances: the comfortable looking on at sport, greyhound racing or the Cup Final at Wembley; the 'one-sided extravagances that are idealism', Billy Graham or the Beatles; the 'images of one's displeasure', the Jews or the Reds or the Limeys.

Finally Musil makes a most prophetic analysis in his portrayal of the young proto-Nazi, Hans Sepp, who with his girl-friend, Gerda, occupy the 'frontier district between the super-rational and the sub-rational'.

"And while faith, having been organised into the system of theological reason, everywhere has to fight a hard battle against doubt and opposition from the rational attitude prevailing nowadays, it seems in fact that the naked fundamental experience — peeled out of all this traditional terminological husks of faith, detached from the old religious concepts — this fundamental experience that perhaps cannot even any longer be called an exclusively religious one, this experience of mystic rapture, has extended vastly and now constitutes the soul of that multiform, irrational movement which haunts the age in which we live like a nocturnal bird that has strayed into the daylight." (p.309)

Do we not here hold in our hands the clue to contemporary unrest among youth: the demand for fundamental experience, 'peeled of all the traditional terminological husk of faith', for 'mystic rapture'? Do not hippies and students on the campus bear out the truth of this diagnosis of a novelist-historian speaking out of his far-sighted foresight?

Heimito von Döderer was born near Vienna in 1896, sixteen years later than Musil; he died in 1966. As a very young man von Döderer fought in the First World War, became a prisoner-of-war in 1916 and thereafter spent several years in Siberia as a lumberjack. On his return home he studied history at the University of Vienna and then pursued his career as a freelance writer of poetry and fiction. He served in the German Air Force during the Second World War, and his major work, at which he laboured for thirty years, is *The Demons*,[6] which first appeared in 1956.

This immense novel has as its focal point the year 1927. On 15 July 1927 riots occurred in Vienna, and the Palace of Justice was burnt out as a consequence of demonstrations against a certain judicial verdict which had resulted in the acquittal of those supposed to be responsible for the shooting of a small boy at Schattendorf earlier that year during a confrontation between Democratic Socialists and pro-Hungarian elements of the Burgenland. Largely through the eyes of Georg von Geyrenhof, a retired civil servant, we are given a picture in depth of Viennese society in the twenties with penetrating insights into academic, political, financial and low-life quarters. In one way or another these are all eventually shown to have a connection with the events of 15 July and with much else besides, namely the state of Central Europe in the twentieth century as a whole, the forging of history in the subtle, complex relationships between individual life-styles and decisions and the process of the collective life of a society. The examples from von Döderer's novel which now follow are designed once again to show what lies behind 'the reverbatory power of facts' and to suggest how the historian can make use of this 'third dimension' of his field of study.

The narrator of the story, Georg von Geyrenhof (how far may he be equated with his creator, like Ulrich with Musil?) lets the reader into his confidence immediately by explaining the reason for his early retirement from professional life: "I shall explain frankly by saying that in the Republic that emerged from the war the life and work of a civil servant seemed to me to have lost much of its raison d'être, whereas in the Old Empire, an Austrian government official was in many cases performing a real function." (p.5)

In other words the traditional Austrian bureaucracy felt itself emasculated in the new type of government inaugurated by the Social Democratic Republic.

He continues:

"Moreover, during the year 1926 my financial situation had changed fundamentally. This change was connected with the release of the securities and bank accounts of Austrian citizens which during the war had been confiscated — or as it was called 'sequestrated' in England. I had shares in certain

Pennsylvanian steel companies deposited in England. By the
Act of Sequestration of 1914 these shares were converted
into British War Bonds . . . now they were restored to me
after a long drawnout and complicated process. . . ." (p.5)

In a flash the author has skilfully opened up the reader's
imagination to those financial perspectives of international
finance which later on were to loom so large in European
history with the failure of the Kreditanstalt Bank of Vienna
in 1929.

Next the reader is introduced to the members of "our
crowd", to which Georg himself belongs and the activities of
which he records and studies as they tend to congregate in
the suburb of Döbling. The following passage defines with
beautiful clarity the historian's fundamental concern:

"You need only draw a single thread at any point you choose
out of the fabric of life and the run will make a pathway
across the whole, and down that wider pathway each of the
other threads will become successively visible, one by one.
For the whole is contained in the smallest segment of
anyone's life-story: (cf. Schrodinger's concept, pp.84-5)
indeed we may even say that it is contained in every single
moment; start up your dredging machine and you take it all
up, no matter whether ecstasy, despair, boredom, or triumph
happens to fill the moving buckets on this endless chain of
ticking seconds." (p.7)

For example, if we 'start up our dredging machine' into
the personal story of any one of the Verney family, that
'single thread' can lead us surely into a deep understanding of
the complex issues of England's great seventeenth-century
conflict between Roundhead and Cavalier where problem
becomes mystery. (Rose Macaulay's *They Were Defeated*[7]
gives comparable access through fiction to the fact of that
great constitutional dispute.) The idea receives further elaboration:

"The past masses like clouds to the right and left of your
head, as it were, and the sharp and sweet tooth of memory
sinks to the heart's core. Out of that past there floats towards
you, as though composed of mists, all that combines to form
the truth; [Ranke's 'things as they actually were'] things we

were scarcely aware of now join themselves together, one related image to another. This forms *a bridge across time,* although in life they may never have touched, may have existed in different years, at different places, so that between them no really traversible pathway of circumstances is visible." (p.13)

The 'single thread' in *The Demons* is the character of Financial Counsellor Levielle, whom in the List of Principal Characters the author quite bluntly labels 'the villain'. Certainly it is through the gradual detection of his designs and villainies that we eventually obtain an understanding of the 'wider pathway' of the other threads. We obtain through words put into the mouth of Réne von Stangeler ("the Ensign — a brilliant young historian", perhaps another aspect of von Döderer himself) a biting critique of a certain section of cultivated Viennese society, which somehow sold the pass to the Austrian form of totalitarianism:

"Such nice cultivated and intellectual people — with beautiful libraries. The amazing thing is how those people manage to keep intelligence at bay. As soon as they smell it, they are against it." (p.49)

Another of the novel's characters, Herr Neuberg, also an historian, delivers himself of the following views: (pp.108ff.)

"All serious and proper study of history must necessarily aim 'at the bull's eye of the present' (as a greater mind than mine has said): one's sights must never deviate from the present. Indeed this is the only purpose of historical studies: to confer a still higher reality upon the present."

"But I should almost think," sayd Frau Ruthmeyr ("an immensely wealthy widow"), "that according to you, Herr Neuberg, we must regard history as we do our own pasts, in the same light, and then it all derives its meaning only from the present."

"Quite so," said Neuberg . . . "That is precisely the way you must regard history, like an extension of your own past. . . . Every age has its own preferences from among preceding periods, and we call these preferences the Renaissance or Romanticism or Classicism or what have you. Whole nations and cultural groups at times live close to some such segment in the past, far closer than they do to recent events . . ." [Is that why there were long queues for the Tutenkhamun and Chinese Exhibitions in London in 1973?] "Gestures and modes of feeling and thinking return, and even ways of looking at the landscape will be revivals of past attitudes. Yet each time the resurrected vision seems entirely new and fresh — and is felt as such. For real repetitions do not exist. Each time the entire past must be re-arranged and sifted anew, since each time the centre of gravity, which governs the direction of the whole, has been displaced, that is, to a different present, and simultaneously means a different, deeply related, and extremely contemporary part of the past. . . . No, the past is nothing fixed; we are always creating it anew. The tremendous masses of its facts are nothing, our conception of them everything." (p.123)

Around the character of Leonard Kakabsa ("a young factory worker who educates himself") is built a study of certain elements among the newly influential working-class of Vienna with their arrogant airs and contempt for intelligence.

"For it was intelligence itself that aroused their antagonism, not at all superior economic position, which at this time was no longer bound up with intelligence — quite the contrary. For intelligence had failed — here lay the real core, the true and bitter root of their antagonism. Intelligence had not been able to prevent the World War and its unfortunate conclusion. Intellectuals with their gift for language had done the talking for the inarticulate people. And they had spoken evilly, had preached madness. Afterwards a general hatred for every kind of authority erupted."

What a convincing diagnosis this is of the whole European malaise, the anti-authoritarian mood of the twenties swinging to an extreme and then provoking the totalitarian authoritarianism of the thirties!

By means of another character, Ederl, the painting contractor, we are given a reminder of the intricate, often shady, dealings between the victorious Allies at the end of the First World War and the defeated Austrians and, by prospective inference, of similar dealings after 1945.

"We might devote a whole chapter of Ederl's biography to

the business he had done with various foreign military missions after the First World War, when they came to set up their offices and apartments. New offices and apartments have to be furnished; they have to be decorated, and a good many such jobs came Ederl's way. Such clients paid their bills in the solid currencies of the victor currencies, and could be charged stiff prices besides. What was more, foreign agencies did not bother to inform Austrian tax bureaus of their payment to Austrian citizens." (pp.137-8)

In a chapter headed "In the East" von Döderer gives us an intimate glimpse of the Austro-Hungarian minorities problem in the Burgenland. In essence this consisted of traditional Magyar repression of the German inhabitants of this area, which when it became part of Austria in 1919 continued to be the scene of Hungarian attempts at intervention, although in the end it remained part of Austria. The connection is established (p.536) between this general problem and the characters of the novel in preparation for the eventual climax of the Vienna riots of 15 July 1927. Csmarits, the disabled veteran "had just come from Schattendorf, which lies close by the Hungarian border. Asked about 'conditions down there', he made a few remarks which suggested casual sympathy with the Socialists, alternated however by a general scepticism which probably sank rather deep in a person whom the so-called course of history had already cost an eye. A man of this sort is not prepared to tear out the other one voluntarily for the sake of any cause whatever. Deep within him is an inexpungeable suspicion that all the people who shout slogans are really aiming at our eyes, whether they are socialists or the one-time authorised representatives of His Majesty's government (six of one and half a dozen of the other). Still and all, Csmarits was a member of the Republican Protection Association. It may be that down there in the Burgenland membership in this private army of the socialists was unavoidable."

Here is another typical illustration of how the novelist can direct our attention to the relationship, often fortuitous, between individual quirk and collective pressure. For in this case 'Uncle' Csmarits and little Pepi Grosser were to be the more or less innocent victims of the Schattendorf incident.

Here (p.581) is a description of a meeting between Leonard and his friend Nicki with one Alois Gail:

"The conversation turned to politics. That was a subject ready to hand in the Burgenland in those days. . . . Nowadays we can scarcely imagine how, given the tremendous political tensions prevailing in Austria at that time, such questions could have been discussed in so relaxed a manner between persons of such differing views — this only nine years after 1918, when the dominant brand of socialism was still a young and struggling faith. In 1926 so-called 'ideologies' were still real opinions and convictions far more than they are to-day, when these hollow forms must serve not only as instruments for personal advancement (which is not so bad) but also as screens for not quite normal emotions."

Behind these last quiet few words does there not lie a vital clue to the motivations of these millions who flocked into one or other of the totalitarian camps?

"And not a year was to pass from the day in the fall of 1926 that Gail and the young men drank and talked so easily at Frauenkirchen to the time when freedom was denied for the first time in Vienna, when its very existence was no longer recognised." (p.583)

This reference is to the judicial verdict of acquittal and the uprising of 15 July 1927. Here von Döderer permits himself a significant author's aside (p.633):

"People, by the way, who commit crimes justifiable by 'ideologies' present a shabby picture compared to professional hardened criminals, whose lives at best exemplify the qualities of solitude, resolution and courage. [Cf. here the character of the criminal Meisgeier in *The Demons* and Moosbrugger in *The Man Without Qualities.*] The others hide their actions behind numbers, are carried along by the crowd, and their deeds are in large part not their own — in contrast to those of the professional criminal — but more reflections of the doings of others.

"The poor victims of that year 1927, including little Pepi, were the first to die in a forest so enormous that nowadays we can no longer see it for all the trees. It has long since grown over our heads. There we have the secret of callousness. . . .

"The Schattendorf case was tried in Vienna more than five months after the event, on 14 July 1927. . . . The jury then voted in favour of the defendants [i.e. the Veterans or anti-socialists]. On the following day 15 July 1927 a spontaneous demonstration — the Social Democratic leadership had no hand in it — brought the workers marching into the heart of the city. They did not march because the murderers of a child and a war veteran were getting off scot-free, but because the child had been a worker's child and the veteran a worker. The 'masses' were demanding class justice, against which their leaders had so often cried out. The people stormed against the verdict of a people's court, against their own verdict. That broke the backbone of freedom: from that point it was maintained in Austria for only a short time, and artificially. The so-called masses have always been fond of settling in a compact group upon the branches of the tree of liberty which tower into infinity. But they must saw off these branches: they cannot help themselves; and then the whole crown of the tree collapses. Sit where he will, the man who listens to the masses has already lost his freedom. The police unfortunately attempted to break up the demonstration: they routed the marchers from the broad Ringstrasse. That same afternoon the Palace of Justice went up in flames." (p.635)

On p.987 there is an excellent analysis of the difference between a police force and a military force, which provides a clear indication of how in Austria the former was gradually superseded by the latter. Here we have the true voice of the 'third dimension' of history speaking, with fiction providing us with a real understanding of how Austrian Nazism eventually came about. It occurs in connection with the policeman, young Karl Zeitler, who is a victim of the riots of 15 July:

"His father was a 'certified holder', such was the term for police officials of the lower ranks who, having completed their term of service in the police, were entitled to a salaried civilian post. In the latter post he had won promotion and then retired. His son, Karl Zeitler, who had also served in the glorious and Royal Imperial Austrian Army had a special way, earnest and emphatic, of speaking of the 'comradeship' of the force. To his mind, comradeship was the heart and soul of the service. The same opinion was held by the Viennese police commissioners' office — and is held to this day. But we must keep in mind, lest we endow those times with ideas arising from a latter time, that the police force then was no military organisation. We have in the meanwhile known a good many types of police forces, which grew more and more to resemble the military, until ultimately the difference between a hundred soldiers and a hundred policemen virtually vanished. And yet this difference is fundamental. A hundred policemen are one hundred individual officials acting with full responsibility, even though occasionally they may obey an unified command. But a hundred or two hundred soldiers are always a single body moved by its head, the captain: a syntagora as the ancient Greeks called it; not a sum of individuals, but a being of a higher, though not more sublime order which incorporates the individual. Hence its impetus, its brute force. In 1927, however, the Viennese police were still devoted to the pure idea of a police force. They were entirely an instrument of peace, a corps of responsible individuals, although well-trained in the use of arms. They lacked the uncompromising either/or of the military, the smashing destructive effect. In those days a police force was not there to suppress; in those days the police were still guardians of the peace. But to their misfortune, the door to a new age was just then turning on its hinges. And it opened in July 1927, while the flames leapt out of the windows of the Palace of Justice: a hot summer day with not wind enough to transform the smoke into streamers."

Here is a passage which compares most interestingly with Musil's diagnosis of the sickness of our times: it is a note jotted down by the Bank Director, Edouard Altschul: "the much praised strong, modern man, in truth so much infected by his own efficiency that his weakness . . . [makes him a Man Without Qualities!] That's what it all comes down to. There you have the source of what might be called our habitual nausea. . . . You see, Vienna has taught me that."

A little later, when the philosopher, Scolander, has joined Altschul and Georg von Geyrenhof in their discussion, there is an arresting passage about Germany and its distinctiveness among European nations.

"In Germany, especially Western Germany, where I come from, you know, people are far more aware than they are here that books, if I may put it so, are as necessary as groceries. This is why the Germans will never quite submerge themselves in their enormous industriousness."

"No, I don't think they will either," said Scolander. "The Germans save themselves from their intellect, while the Austrians do the same with their vital juices. Each has his own way. Only the future will demonstrate who comes out better in this test: that is to say, who retains more of his humanity. In both cases the sources of error are inordinate, for only both forms of reaction taken together could really be called intelligence." (p.1150)

Now the historian of modern Europe is of course enormously concerned with 'who came out best' after the twenties, namely in the thirties, forties and fifties and, in making his historical judgement, 'intellect' (German) and 'vital juices' (Austrian) afford him useful clues. Von Döderer passes a historical judgement about the events of 15 July:

"This was the most important moment in the history of the Vienna police force since the First World War. The police had necessarily become armed troops (an irreversible process), closed formations which advanced in order, firing and driving everybody before them." (p.1261)

In dealing with the abortive attack on the University by the 'undisciplined, reckless elements' there is a most penetrating analysis of the very stuff of that socio-political malaise which heralds the breakdown of traditionally democratic forms of government:

"Their assault was by no means directed against the intellectuals — as was assumed by the people talking in the buffet, who thereby shed some light on themselves. Rather, at bottom, the provocation had been a smell; for no sphere of the senses reaches so far out into the hereafter in the here as that of smell; often it is no longer perceived with the nose, and yet it exists, and it is a veritable smell. In this case, the hostility of the workers was directed towards the regional stable odour in the University towards the 'provincialism' of those who studied here, towards a conservative temper held not because it had been sought and rewon, but which was 'held' because it had been hung on to and never lost. Such a hold on tradition can be a source of a host of respectable errors, and the more respectable the errors are, the worse they are; compared to such errors, all vices (which after all, being marked with filth, proclaim their nature) are more harmless scribblings by the hands of fools. The 'intellectuals' foregathered here had already descended, from that platform on which the historically-acting man stands, precisely as many steps as those assailants outside when they plunged into the vat of the masses, which dissolves everything and breaks all chemical ties, sending some to the right and others to the left, as the customary classification goes. All roads of descent lead down, but never do people hate one another so passionately as when they choose different downward paths. Such downward paths may not even run together in the void, in nihilism; for then something would be revealed for all to see which must be concealed — or at least, the concealment of which seems to be the sole and ultimate goal of the struggle." (pp.1272-3)

Finally (p.1311) referring to 15 July 1927: "Thus ended for us the day which quite incidentally signified the Cannae of Austrian freedom. But no one knew that at the time, we least of all."

Two general observations are in place here: first, that von Döderer with his witch-cult and mediaeval cut-back at the castle of Neudegg evidently found it necessary, as did Thomas Mann in his *Dr Faustus* with his historical excursion into the past, to approach the problem of evil in twentieth-century terms by a distancing technique, that is, using a late medieval perspective to bring into focus an otherwise inconceivable contemporary reality. Secondly, it should be clearly realised that what has here been distilled from the bulky text of a long and distinguished work of art is only what could be of use to an historian of the period. It does not and cannot attempt to do any kind of justice to *The Demons* as a fine novel in its own right, composed of a masterly plot and studded with an array of entertaining characters.

In conclusion I would like to consider Herman Melville's

story, *Benito Cereno*[8] as it provides the psycho-historian with a fine instrument for the interpretation of at least two major historical phenomena, totalitarianism and racial strife. To make this clear, it will be necessary to begin by briefly summarising the plot.

In the year 1799 Captain Amasa Delano of Massachusetts was anchored in his trading vessel off the coast of Chile: into the waters where he lay sailed a vessel, the *San Dominick*, flying no colours and proceeding somewhat aimlessly and, because of the proximity of reefs, rather perilously. The good-natured Delano decided to make contact with it, and, as he approached this strange ship, he noticed that its appearance suggested that of a Spanish merchantman, carrying negro slaves but presenting a neglected and battered condition. Climbing on board, he quickly learnt from the crew of white and black men pressing around him that scurvy had swept off a great part of their number, more especially the Spaniards, and that they had narrowly escaped shipwreck in a storm off Cape Horn. His eye was next caught by the Spanish captain of the *San Dominick*, Don Benito Cereno, a woebegone young man in soiled but rich apparel and by Babo, a black attendant physically supporting him with a fawning and menial look. Delano greeted his fellow captain and brought on board fresh supplies of food and drink for those on the distressed vessel. Gradually, however, the odd behaviour of Don Benito Cereno, and the obsequious but sinister attentions paid to him by Babo, filled the American's heart and mind with a distinct unease. This was compounded by a series of suspicious incidents, such as secret signals passing between members of the crew and violent brawls between blacks and whites. However, with the rising of a long-awaited breeze, Delano took charge of the *San Dominick* and helped to sail her into the harbour, where she came to anchor not far off from Delano's own ship. Then just as he was taking leave of Don Benito and was already sitting in the whale boat come to fetch him, the tottering Spaniard suddenly leapt over the bulwarks of the *San Dominick* into the rowing boat below, instantly followed by Babo. Violence broke out, in which Babo, having tried unsuccessfully to stab Don Benito, was overcome by the American sailors and securely fastened. The black crew on the *San Dominick* weighed anchor and started to sail away, but Delano's men went in pursuit, and after a bloody fight overcame the blacks and took control of their ship. The two vessels under the supervision of Delano then sailed back to the port of Lima. Here there was an official investigation, which revealed that there had been a mutiny by the blacks while at sea, who had forced Don Benito to do their bidding and who had nearly succeeded in tricking Captain Delano. Babo was executed, and Don Benito Cereno, an utterly broken man, died a few months later in a monastic mountain retreat.

Now the first thing for the psycho-historian to note is the chronology of the tale, published by Melville in 1855 and with its action set in 1799. Its implications, however, stretch back into the past of the original slave trade and early Spanish imperialism and forward into the future of twentieth-century black power and totalitarianism. In other words, the subject matter, although located in a particular place and time, is spread out across time and must be sought on the bridge across that span of time. An examination of the deeper aspects of the story will reveal the nature of the subject matter, but first a further piece of psychological elucidation is required.

In blunt recapitulation of the psychological hypothesis set out already (in Chapter III), this is simply the fact that every individual has a dark, largely unconscious side to his personality, his shadow, that each society has a correspondingly dark, largely unconscious side to itself, and that both have a collective, archetypal shadow, corresponding in Jungian terms to mankind's instinctual life, his 'Saurian tail'. Without this shadow the individual and the species can have no knowledge of themselves, of who they really are; the black is needed to define the white, as Jesus needed Judas Iscariot, but only a high degree of consciousness can prevent the former from being swallowed up by the later, and ensure an equipoise being maintained.

Melville's story strikes a reverberating note right at the beginning: "Shadows present, foreshadowing deeper shadows to come" (p.3), Babo as the shadow of Don Benito, the negro crew of the *San Dominick* as the shadow of the white race, the whole darkly sinister atmosphere on board, sensed dimly but not properly, consciously understood by Captain Delano.

The latter is himself an almost Parsifal-like innocent type until the rude events of mutiny shock him into conscious realisation of the truth of the situation.

"But the temper of my mind that morning was more than commonly pleasant, while the sight of so much suffering — more apparent than real — added to my good nature, compassion and charity, happily interweaving the three. Had it been otherwise, doubtless, as you hint, some of my interferences with the blacks might have ended unhappily enough. Besides that, those feelings I spoke of enabled me to get the better of momentary distrust, at times when acuteness might have cost me my life, without saving another's. Only at the end did my suspicions get the better of me, and you know how wide of the mark they then proved." (pp.103-4)

Delano is referring to his wrongful suspicion of Don Benito. There are a few lines of dialogue, which, with a fine touch of irony, comment through the persons of Don Benito and Babo on the relationship, fateful for good and ill, between the black and white races. Cereno speaks:
"But it is Babo here to whom, under God, I owe not only my own preservation, but likewise to him, chiefly, the merit is due of pacifying his more ignorant brethren, when at intervals tempted to murmurings.'
'Ah, master,' sighed the black, bowing his face, 'don't speak of me; Babo is nothing; what Babo has done was but duty.'
'Faithful fellow,' cried Captain Delano. 'Don Benito, I envy you such a friend; slave I cannot call him.'
As master and man stood before him, the black upholding the white, Captain Delano could not but bethink him of the beauty of that relationship which could present such a spectacle of fidelity on the one hand and confidence on the other." (pp.18-19)

In the mind of good Captain Delano there was nothing but innocent satisfaction at the evidence of black-white co-operation, for he was still ignorant at that stage that there had been a mutiny and that the blacks were really in control of the *San Dominick*. A little later, witnessing Don Benito's feeble and ineffective attempt to control the assault of a black member of his crew on a white: "Is it," thought Captain Delano, "that this helpless man is one of those paper captains, I've known, who by policy wink at what by power they cannot put down? I know no sadder sight than a commander who has little of command but the name." (p.22)

The 'paper captain' may well be understood as a potent symbol of the ineffectiveness of a weak democracy before a totalitarian challenge — Brünning before Hitler in Weimar Germany — or the retreat of white power before black in Africa and the USA.

Next there is that wonderful scene between Don Benito, Babo, Delano and Atufal ('the pretended rebel, but powerful shadow'), that gigantic black, in which the Spanish captain tries in vain to make Atufal beg pardon for an offence he had committed.

"An iron collar was about his neck, from which depended a chain, thrice wound round his body; the terminating links padlocked together at a broad band of iron, his girdle.

"How like a mute Atufal moves," murmured the servant.

The black mounted the steps of the poop, and, like a brave prisoner, brought up to receive sentence, stood in unquailing muteness before Don Benito, now recovered from his attack.

At the first glimpse of his approach, Don Benito had started, a resentful shadow swept over his face; and, as with the sudden memory of bootless rage, his white lips glued together.

"This is some mulish mutineer," thought Captain Delano, surveying, not without a mixture of admiration, the colossal form of the negro.

"See, he awaits your question, master," said the servant.

Thus reminded, Don Benito, nervously averting his glance, as if shunning, by anticipation, some rebellious response, in a disconcerted voice, thus spoke:

"Atufal, will you ask my pardon now?"

The black was silent.

"Again, master," murmured the servant, with bitter up-braiding eyeing his countryman; "Again, master, he will bend to master yet."

"Answer," said Don Benito, still averting his glance. "Say

but the one word PARDON, and your chains shall be off."

Upon this, the black, slowly raising both arms, let them lifelessly fall, his links clanking, his head bowed; as much as to say, "No, I am content."

"Go," said Don Benito, with inkept and unknown emotion.

Deliberately, as he had come, the black obeyed.

"Excuse me, Don Benito," said Captain Delano, "but this scene surprises me; what means it, pray?"

"It means that that negro alone, of all the band, has given me peculiar cause of offence. I have put him in chains; I . . ." Here he paused; his hand to his head, as if there were a swimming there, or a sudden bewilderment of memory had come over him; but meeting his servant's kindly glance, seemed reassured, and proceeded: "I could not scourge such a form. But I told him he must ask my pardon. As yet he has not. At my command, every two hours he stands before me."

"And how long has this been?"

"Some sixty days."

"And obedient in all else? And respectful?"

"Yes."

"Upon my conscience then," exclaimed Captain Delano, impulsively, "he has a royal spirit in him, this fellow."

"He may have some right to it," bitterly returned Don Benito; "he says he was king in his own land."

"Yes," said the servant, entering a word, "those slits in Atufal's ears once held wedges of gold; but poor Babo here, in his own land, was only a poor slave; a blackman's slave was Babo, who now is the white's."

Somewhat annoyed by these conversational familiarities, Captain Delano turned curiously upon the attendant, then glanced inquiringly at his master; but, as if long wonted to these little informalities, neither master nor man seemed to understand him.

"What, pray, was Atufal's offence, Don Benito?" asked Captain Delano; "if it was not something very serious, take a fool's advice, and in view of his general docility, as well as in some natural respect for his spirit, remit his penalty."

"No, no, master, never will do that," here murmured the servant to himself, "proud Atufal must first ask master's pardon. The slave there carries the padlock, but master here carries the key."

His attention thus directed, Captain Delano now noticed for the first time that, suspended by a slender, silken cord, from Don Benito's neck hung a key. At once, from the servant's muttered syllables divining the key's purpose, he smiled and said: "So, Don Benito — padlock and key — significant symbols, truly."

Biting his lip, Don Benito faltered.

Though the remark of Captain Delano, a man of such native simplicity as to be incapable of satire or irony, had been dropped in playful allusion to the Spaniard's singularly evident lordship over the black; yet the hypochondriac seemed in some way to have taken it as a malicious reflection upon his confessed inability thus far to break down, at least, on a verbal summons, the entrenched will of the slave." (pp.25-7)

Once again, it would seem, the novelist's imagination has succeeded in focusing through Atufal, the padlock and the key, the predicament of white-black relationships, the blacks still manacled, the whites striving ineffectually to obtain reassurance of black subservience, one whole passage seething with the message that white dominance once challenged must eventually collapse. Someone, somewhere, sometime would fit the key to the padlock.

Then there is the gruesome scene in which Captain Delano witnesses the shaving of Don Benito by Babo:

"Setting down his basin, the negro searched among the razors, as for the sharpest, and having found it, gave it an additional edge by expertly stropping it on the firm, smooth, oily skin of his open palm; he then made a gesture as if to begin, but midway stood suspended for an instant, one hand elevating the razor, the other professionally dabbling among the bubbling suds on the Spaniard's lank neck. Not un-affected by the close sight of the gleaming steel, Don Benito nervously shuddered, his usual ghastliness was heightened by the lather, which lather, again, was intensified in its hue by the contrasting sootiness of the negro's body. Altogether the scene was somewhat peculiar, at least to Captain Delano, nor, as he saw the two thus postured, could he resist the vagary, that in the black he saw a headsman, and in the white, a man at the block. But this was one of those antic conceits, appearing and vanishing in a breath, from which, perhaps, the best regulated mind is not free." (pp.58-9)

No, this was no 'antic conceit'; it was a premonition, which could arise in even so well regulated a mind as Captain Delano's, a premonition becoming more and more powerful among twentieth-century men of good will, faced by the early intimations of totalitarianism in Italy and Germany or in the white rulers of South Africa as they recoiled in the face of Sharpeville.

In the closing paragraphs of the tale Melville forces us to stare into the very heart of its mystery:

"I think I understand you; you generalize, Don Benito; and mournfully enough. But the past is passed; why moralize upon it? Forget it. See, yon bright sun has forgotten it all, and the blue sea, and the blue sky; these have turned over new leaves."

"Because they have no memory," he dejectedly replied; "because they are not human."

"But these mild trades that now fan your cheek, Don Benito, do they not come with a human-like healing to you? Warm friends, steadfast friends are the trades."

"With their steadfastness they but waft me to my tomb, Senor," was the foreboding response.

"You are saved, Don Benito," cried Captain Delano, more and more astonished and pained; "you are saved; what has cast such a shadow on you?"

"The negro."

There was silence, while the moody man sat, slowly and unconsciously gathering his mantle, as it were a pall." (pp.104-5)

The innocent Captain Delano cannot understand why Don Benito is not now able to rejoice at his rescue. The Spaniard first makes the point of the difference between man and nature: the latter has no memory, while the former has, his own conscious memory informing him that his experience at the hands of the black mutineers has been a deadly one. Why? Because of the shadow cast upon him by the negro, the unavoidable fate of anyone who instead of integrating the shadow tries to eliminate it or ignore it, the fate of the white races making a similar mistake or the fate of democracies failing to deal integratively with the causes of totalitarianism. (See Chapter VIII: unemployment under Weimar leading to the horrors of Buchenwald.)

Such an exercise as the one just undertaken with Benito Cereno enables us to achieve that 'new dimension of time-study' already referred to in Chapter I. By means of a synthesis of Melville's own character traits, his created characters, the phenomena of race relations and totalitarianism, the psycho-historian can contribute to the record of the growth of human consciousness in this phase of its evolution, which it is his function to do.

8

Germany in Miniature: a Psycho-Historical Study

Determinants of German History

In his inaugural lecture as Professor of History at the University of Jena in the year 1781 Schiller warned his audience against the *'Brotgelebrte'*, the bread-and-butter historian, who fails through 'not entering sympathetically into the activities he describes'. Striving to avoid this fault, I shall on the other hand attempt to meet the challenge contained in the following passage from George Gale's article in the *Spectator* of 8 January 1972:

"We still however await a work of synthetic history which will assemble the relevant facts, let them confront each other, and make it possible to set about formulating more precisely than we have so far been able, or dared, the crucial inter-related problems of identity and responsibility, of history and of myth, as well as those of frontiers and of social order, which are particularly German. The task, although difficult and painful, is most necessary."

German history, being itself part of world history, it is necessary to begin by once again redefining this particular branch of academic studies. History is the record of the growth of human consciousness, and this record consists of two parts: events and the interpretation of events. The former belong to the order of chronological sequence, the later to the viewpoint imposed on them by the historian according to his situation in time and place, and this viewpoint must strive to transcend mere temporal flow. A psycho-history of Germany should therefore concern itself with the record of the growth of individual and collective consciousness among those generations of mankind, who have lived and died in a certain area of the earth's surface roughly classifiable as central Europe. We shall deal with events such as the Peace of Augsburg, and we shall also be involved in such interpretations of the German past as the philosopher, psychologist and novelist may have to offer. At one and the same moment we shall be striving to understand the determinants of German history within their timebound incidence and in their chronologically overlapping phases, and even in some cases in their altogether timeless qualities. What we are after in these German studies in depth is the effect of historical time as somehow contained in a timeless present.

The Events of a Thousand Years, c. AD 800-1800

North of the Danube and east of the Rhine various German tribes were stared at across the waters by Roman legionaries of the Empire. There had been an occasion on which such tribes had slaughtered Varus and his legions in the Teutonberger Wald in AD 9, but as Tacitus described them in his *Germania* they remained for the most part outside the Roman *Limes*. It is not without significance for our own days that even at the time of the greatest extension of the Roman Empire eastwards, *c.*100, certain territories later to be regarded as part of modern Germany never felt the civilising mission of Rome. With the decline of the Roman Empire from the fifth century, no central form of government existed in central Europe, while the indigenous tribes were beginning to feel ever-strengthening pressures on them from attacking hordes coming out of Asia.

It is with the establishment of the Carolingian Empire in the ninth century, its recognition by the Eastern Empire in 812, and the Treaty of Verdun in 843 that the story of Germany proper may be thought of as originating. For by that treaty Europe was divided into three parts, the future kingdom of France in the west, the future Germany in the east, and Lotharingia, the 'middle kingdom', in between. There were already at work factors which were to give a different shape to German history as compared with other countries. First, there was the unusual strength of the German feudal baronage, insisting on its right to elect its own *primus inter pares,* the German monarch — no sovereign ruler he; secondly there was the barons' hard-won and dearly cherished independence of action as defenders of the Eastern marches against invaders from still further East, the Margraves. Modern Prussia was once the Mark of Brandenburg. From among the particularist groupings of Saxons, Franconians, Bavarians, Bohemians, the first man to be chosen as German monarch was Conrad of Franconia.

As he lay dying, he nominated his successor, Henry I (919-36), Henry the Fowler as he came to be known because of his hunting exploits. "I know that no man is worthier to sit on my throne than my enemy Henry of Saxony. . . . When I am dead, take him the crown and the sacred lance, the golden armlet, the sword, and the purple mantle of the old kings."

It was this Henry who first put a serious stop to the ten-year-old series of invasions of the German heartlands by the Hungarians. He ordered a dead dog to be thrown at the envoy's feet: "In future this is all your master will get from us," and his policy of building strong 'burgs' as defensive ramparts proved him right.

His son, Otto I, reigned from 936 to 973. Although largely successful in quelling the claims of his fellow-barons, he began to experience the struggle, which was so largely to dominate medieval European politics of the eleventh and twelfth centuries, namely that between Emperor and Pope. He and his successors were lured into trying to make good their claim and pretension not only to dominate the Church ecclesiastically by nominating bishops but also to assert their political claims south of the Alps. In February 962 Otto I became Holy Roman Emperor, temporal overlord of Christendom with the Papacy in the eyes of Europe merely the chief see of the Emperor's dominions. This struggle, known as the Investiture Contest, culminated in the struggle between the Emperor, Henry IV (1056-1106) and Pope Gregory VII. In spite of the former's forced humiliation at Canossa in 1077, victory on the whole rested with the Emperor in the intermittent wars that raged at this time between the supporters of either side. Yet, although Henry IV outlived Gregory by twenty-one years, the combination of his own sons and subsequent popes proved too strong for him; he was cast into prison and died of neglect. In 1122 the Concordat of Worms arrived at a compromise: rulers were to renounce their claim to invest bishops and abbots with ring and crozier, but the ceremony at which this took place must be in the presence of the king or his representative to whom the new bishop or abbot must at once do homage for his lands and offices.

When the Emperor Henry IV crossed the ice-bound Alps on his journey of submission to Canossa, he was accompanied by a faithful knight, Frederick of Buren, who married his daughter. Their son was elected Emperor as Conrad III (1137-52), the first of the Hohenstaufen. They were also called 'Waiblingen', while their chief rival, the House of Bavaria, was called 'Welf': the feud between them convulsed Germany, and when it spread to Italy became known as the war between Ghibelline and Guelph. Frederick I (1153-90), the Barbarossa of the Third Crusade, was a Hohenstaufen on his father's side, a Welf on his mother's, and for a while there were hopes of a reconciliation between the warring factions, but Frederick's imperialist ambitions ruled that out until he had suffered a severe reverse at the hands of the Italian communes in 1176 at the Battle or Legnano. Yet subsequently he succeeded in asserting his authority over Henry the Lion in Brunswick and gradually began to appear as something more than first among his peers: he became a king supported by the Church and is still looked back to as real founder of the German sense of nationality. Frederick Barbarossa bound Germany to her southern neighbours by marrying his eldest son, Henry, to Constance, heiress of the Norman kingdoms of Sicily and Naples, thus aiming to create a permanent Hohenstaufen counterpoise in the south to the alliance of the Pope and the Guelph towns in the north. After Frederick's death in Asia Minor, his son, Henry VI (1190-97) pursued a fierce policy towards his Sicilian possessions and aimed at creating a permanent, hereditary Hohenstaufen rule based on the south of Italy. However he died at the early age of thirty-two and his small son, the King of Naples, was bequeathed by his mother Constance, before she too died, to the care of Pope Innocent III. This mighty character proceeded to try and make good an absolute papal claim to supremacy.

"The Lord Jesus Christ has set up one ruler over all things as the Universal Vicar, and as all things in Heaven, Earth and

Hell bow the knee to Christ, so should all obey Christ's Vicar that there be but one flock and shepherd." And to the young Frederick he remarked: "God has not spared the rod. He has taken away your father and mother; yet he has given you a worthier father, His Vicar, and a better mother, the Church."

For a while after Henry VI's death there was a disputed succession to the emperorship, but in the end Pope Innocent III gave his support to the young king of Naples, who then became Emperor in 1215 and reigned until 1250 as Frederick II.

In 1216 Pope Innocent III died, and the twenty-year-old Emperor emerged as the dominating figure of central and southern Europe, but he clung to his Naples base for reasons of personal taste and showed little enthusiasm to fulfil his vow of going on a crusade. Pope Gregory IX decided to challenge him and began by excommunicating him. In spite of this he did eventually capture Jerusalem, while the struggle between Pope and Emperor continued in a series of debilitating wars, and the foundations of royal authority which had been laid by Barbarossa and Henry VI were undermined. Emperor Frederick II may have been *Stupor Mundi* but he certainly did not contribute to the growth of German nationhood.

After his death there was a period of disputed rulerships throughout the German lands, the 'Great Interregnum' of 1256-73, but with the election of Rudolf of Habsburg as Emperor in 1273, a turning-point in German medieval history was reached because after that date the fatal lure from south of the Alps lapsed, and the Empire could begin to concentrate to the north of them. During the thirteenth and fourteenth centuries the most creative energies of the German people were released in cities such as Augsburg and Nuremberg, in the great Hanseatic trading companies and in the campaigns of the Teutonic knights in Prussia. It was during the reign of the Emperor Charles IV (1347-78) that there was issued in 1356 the Golden Bull, important because it laid down the rules by which imperial elections were in future to be conducted. There were to be seven Electors, three archbishops and four laymen, all of them accorded tremendous privileges which elevated them above the other territorial princes. who were merely represented in the

Imperial Diet or Parliament. The Electors became a kind of feudal oligarchy with strangleholds on any more general and liberal developments which persisted until 1806.

Thus by the beginning of the sixteenth century, Germany as part of the medieval Holy Roman Empire had not developed nationalist attributes but was divided into territorial states ruled by hereditary princes. Throughout the period of the German Reformation the Emperor was a Habsburg, Charles V (1519-58), to whose interests those of the territorial princes were sacrificed. Already in the fifteenth century there had been mutterings of protest from a discontented German peasantry against degenerate Catholic practices of administration, led by one Hans Bohm.

It is against the background of both these factors that the career of Martin Luther (1483-1546) must be viewed. His own personality felt the need for salvation, culminating in the doctrine of justification by faith. The factors of his socio-political alignment with several of the German territorial princes in their efforts to assert their own independent standing against Charles V, his coming under the ban of the Papacy after the Diet of Worms in 1521, and then his brief identification with the cause of the peasants in the Peasants' War of 1524-5, and the spread of his ideas by the recently available printed word and hymn singing were to bring him into the secular camp of the German princes, particularly Philip of Hesse, and to align him more and more with a kind of state Protestantism: Lutheranism became "not the emblem of revolt but the badge of princely protection and authority".[1]

At the Diet of Spires in 1526 Lutheran princes obtained, as a temporary concession, the right of regulating religious affairs within their own territories, and this was the thin end of the wedge. It led on to the substitution of hereditary Lutheran lands for elective Catholic estates, marked by the successful protest of the Lutheran princes against the attempt made in 1529 by Charles V to reverse the process. The Augsburg Confession of 1530 followed, an attempt at compromise by Philip Malancthon, but when this failed, intrigues, rebellions and wars ensued from 1530 to 1555 with Lutheranism "crystallising into evangelical conservatism".[2] Finally in 1555 came the settlement known as the Peace of Augsburg based on the principle of '*Cujus regio-ejus religio*', a formula which was to harass German political and cultural life till well into the twentieth century. By means of it the Lutheran princes were given the right to expel dissentients and to retain all ecclesiastical property that had been secularized before 1552. At Augsburg were sown the seeds of the Thirty Years' War (1618-48).

This was a religious and economic struggle within the German lands, which gradually developed into a dynastic struggle between the competing powers of central Europe, worked on by such outside catalysts as Gustavus Adolphus of Sweden and Richelieu of France. By the time it ended with the Treaty of Westphalia in 1648, German lands had been so fought over and ravaged, tempers and attitudes so coarsened and frayed, particularisms so entrenched, that it could well be said that the socio-political development of Germany was delayed by over a hundred years. Then, when it began to come, it did so through the rise to pre-eminence of one part, namely Brandenburg Prussia under Frederick William, the Great Elector (1640-88). In the eighteenth century the kingdom of Prussia established itself as the leading German state. The two men chiefly responsible for this were King Frederick William I (1713-40) and Frederick II, the Great (1740-86): the single strongest integrating force was the army. Under the latter's rule Prussia expanded still further: the Seven Years' War and the partition of Poland are evidence of this. Frederick II's friendship with Voltaire, the birth of Goethe in 1748, the glories of German music during this period, help to underline the nature of the split that had been developing more and more deeply between German political and cultural life, the one primitive and retarded, the other exquisitely parochial and at the same time universal. German political history in the nineteenth century was to prove a fateful working out of this grim paradox.

Immanuel Kant (1724-1804) gave philosophical expression to the nature of this paradoxical problem in his efforts to reconcile freedom and order. "The starting point of Kant's thought may have been his hatred of tyranny. But in the effort to render external tyrants unnecessary, the individual was required to impose upon himself an even more rigorous code than the King of Prussia imposed on his subjects. A man

could be allowed to be free only if he was completely subject
to an inner control."[3] This line of thinking, taken in conjunc-
tion with that emphasis on the individuality of people which
distinguishes German political thought for the following
century, must be seen in connection with the powerful
influence of Hegel (1770-1831). He was a member of the
'First Guards Regiment of Learning' at the University of
Berlin and, as Ritter remarked[4]: "His political philosophy is
the most decisive expression of the intellectual movement
which replaced the old connections and ideal of a European
universalism with a ruthless individualisation of the international scene," that is, the worship of the sovereign national
state.

The Interpretations of Psycho-History

"The rise and fall of civilisations in the long, broad course of
history can be seen to have been largely a function of the
integrity and cogency of their supporting canons of myth; for
not authority but aspiration is the motivator, builder and
transformer of civilisation."[5] Let us now take a steady look
at those 'canons of myth' supporting the thousand years of
history we have just swiftly traversed. It is our general thesis
that behind or below and informing the consciously formulated and acted out situations of human activity, it is possible
to detect the unconscious, archetypal forces expressed in
myth and legend. Moreover in all situations where the
channels of conscious expression are, for any reason, inadequate, the less conscious, instinctual forces burst their
banks and flood across the previously drained and dyked
lands of civilisation: there is the regression to an older, less
sophisticated, simpler and even barbaric level of existence.
Always it is possible to observe one simple life-law in
operation: the greater the degree of consciousness, the greater
the need for control; consciousness without control leads to
catastrophe whether in the Teutonic forests of the Dark and
Middle Ages, the plains of seventeenth-century Saxony,
wracked by the Thirty Years' War, or the twilight of the
Weimar Republic.

Our first clue is the Nibelung Lied, only set down about AD
1200 but referring to a much earlier period, probably to the
middle of the sixth century, when the Burgundians, an East

German tribe, settled on the Rhine near Worms. A hundred years later they revolted against the Roman governor, Aetius, and were themselves almost annihilated by the Huns. The great Hun leader, Attila, is the Etzel of the legend, and at once we have to come to terms first with the characters of the original Nibelung Lied and secondly with the recreation of these by Richard Wagner in the middle of the nineteenth century. Below the temporal flow of fifteen hundred years the river-bed of unconscious energy remained constant in the German peoples. How does the old story go?

Siegfried, youngest of the kings of the Netherlands, travelled to Worms to seek the hand in marriage of Kriemhild, sister of Gunther, King of the Burgundians. The latter agreed to the match provided Siegfried would first help him obtain in marriage Brunhilde, Queen of Iceland. She however was only to be had by the man who could beat her in hurling a spear, throwing a huge stone and in leaping. By means of a cloak of invisibility Siegfried, impersonating Gunther, succeeded in those three feats, and subsequently a double marriage took place between Gunther and Brunhilde, Siegfried and Kriemhild. So far so good, but after a time the two erstwhile brides started gossiping together, and Kriemhild boasted to Brunhilde of Siegfried's superior prowess especially as epitomised in his disguised wooing of Brunhilde. That furious lady then hired a warrior of her court, Hagen, to stab Siegfried to death in the back while he was drinking from a brook. Some thirteen years later Kriemhild married again, this time Etzel, King of the Huns, and she planned a horrible vengeance, made all the more necessary in her eyes by Hagen's murder of her own son while he and Brunhilde were visiting the Hun court. With her own hands Kriemhild cut off the heads of Gunther and Hagen, she herself being subsequently slaughtered in turn by one Hildebrand.

Here is a barbaric, pagan tale retold in medieval Christian times, comparable with many other such tales, such as the Volsungen Saga, the Icelandic version of it. It contains the hero figure of Siegfried, the dark shadow figure of Hagen, the primitive, primordial image of woman as personified in Kriemhild and Brunhilde, and it proclaims the barbaric virtues of physical courage and loyalty, together with their

opposites of treachery and cunning with few of the sophis-
tications of later ages in which they were to be decked out.
There is yet another archetypal motif in the Nibelung Lied,
which is the Nibelung hoard of gold and precious stones,
which Siegfried stole from Nibelung land and gave as dowry
to his wife; when he had been murdered by Hagen, it was
seized by the murderer and then sunk for safe keeping in the
Rhine, never to be recovered by Hagen because of his own
assassination.

Out of this legendary material Wagner fashioned his great
music-drama, which constitutes a penetrating analysis chiefly,
though not only, of the condition of the German people of
the 1860s but also of the state of Europe as a whole in the
second half of the nineteenth century. By means of his
poetry and music Wagner revealed mythical, largely unconscious constants underlying the consciously held variables, the gods and goddesses of Valhalla on the one hand,
symbolising super-consciousness but in unsure and imperfect
control of destiny, the dragon and the dwarfs on the other
hand symbolising crude, instinctive life and lust, and the
mortals like Siegmund, Siegfried, Sieglinde and Hagen caught
between the two worlds with the character of Brunhilde,
armoured warrior maiden, as the tragic bridging figure
between them. Wagner's *Ring* was, as we shall be seeing ever
more clearly and in greater detail as we move chronologically
from the nineteenth century into the twentieth, a prophetic
work of art spelling out in majestic operatic melody the law
of consciousness, control or catastrophe — introject the beast
or the bestial will consume you.

Our second clue is the medieval love story of Tristan and
Isolde, itself an European phenomenon, with, as we shall be
seeing, a specific German resonance, and once again a
trans-temporal connection, this time across eight hundred
years or so of chronological sequence. This famous love
story, first fully narrated by Thomas of Brittany between
1165 and 1170, received its classic treatment at the hands of
Gottfried von Strasbourg, who produced his version about
1210. His own words of introduction make clear that the
grand theme of his tale is love and death, the strange intimate
relationship between them portrayed in a European setting,
which was at that time struggling with the problem of Eros

and Agape, courtly and common love, and the whole question of the relationship between the pagan and Christian views of human destiny.

"I have undertaken a labour, a labour out of love for the world and to comfort noble hearts: those that I hold dear, and the world to which my heart goes out. Not the common world do I mean of those who (as I have heard) cannot bear grief and do but desire to bathe in bliss. (May God then let them dwell in bliss!) Their world and manner of life my tale does not regard; its life and mine lie apart. Another world do I hold in mind, which bears together in one heart its bitter-sweet, its dear grief, its heart's delight and its pain of longing, dear life and sorrowful death, its dear death and sorrowful life. In this world let me have my world, to be damned with it, or to be saved."[6]

Here is an affirmation of readiness to suffer the pangs of full consciousness, inevitably caused by the conflict of opposites, and scorn for "those who cannot bear grief and desire but to bathe in bliss". Is it fanciful to perceive in this the poet's sensitive awareness of a common human tendency, exaggerated in the case of Germany, to seek identification with one of the opposites by annihilating the other, the rejection of the middle path? The tragic quality of life demands acceptance of both, not the attempt to have the one without the other. For it is an illusion to believe that consciousness can escape contradiction by identifying with one of its terms: conscious appreciation of Shakespeare's *The Tempest* precludes our identifying with only Prospero or only Caliban. This is a theme which will come up for scrutiny again in the age of Goethe.

The key to Gottfried's interest lies in the phrase, "dear life and sorrowful death — dear death and sorrowful life". This was the statement of a predicament still very much alive to the English mystical poet, Vaughan, who in the seventeenth century was writing about "dear, beauteous death, the jewel of the just". It was given fresh life and meaning by Rilke at the beginning of the twentieth century when he spoke of man's encompassing the Great Death, his own proper death as the fulfilment of his life instead of the futile, meaningless death of the barely conscious mass of mankind.

Now the Great Death has often been thought of as being capable of being experienced in the ecstasy of human love between man and woman, an ecstasy which demands their death to all the other concerns of life, and frequently to their own actual deaths as in the case of Tristan and Isolde. For what, in short, was their fate? Stripping the story of its countless prologues, variations, meanderings and excursions, it is an account of how King Mark of Cornwall sent his favourite knight, Tristan, to procure the hand of Isolde of Ireland in marriage; how Tristan and Isolde fell fatally in love with one another, for which occurrence the love-death potion is the symbol, and how after Isolde's marriage to King Mark that illicit love was discovered by Melot, Tristan was mortally wounded and Isolde died of grief at his deathbed.

> A man, a woman, a woman, a man.
> Tristan Isolt, Isolt Tristan.

"As the glow of love's inward fire increases, so the frenzy of the lovers' suit. But this pain is so full of love, this anguish so enheartening, that no noble heart would dispense with it, once having been so heartened."

"The glow of love's inward fire", elsewhere in Europe more completely sublimated by the Christian church and also possibly finding other outlets in maritime adventure, burnt on in the lives of most Germans, thereby setting them a specially difficult task, namely how to contain that passion without repression or extravagant expression.

> We read their life, we read their death,
> And to us it is sweet as bread.
> Their life, their death, are our bread.
> So lives their life, so lives their death,
> So live they still and yet are dead
> And their death is the bread of the living.

In this passage there is encapsulated a whole philosophy of life to the effect that it is by seeking and then accepting our own, our proper deaths, sometimes as in the case of Tristan and Isolde through being consumed by the passion of sexual love, that there is generated the timeless within the time-bound, Blake's 'eternity in a grain of sand'.

Each age and every individual are confronted with this

challenge to which they make varying, imperfect responses. It was the greatness and the misery of the German Middle Ages through the genius of Gottfried of Strasbourg to recognise and declare the nature of this challenge with particular intensity: the inadequacy of response to it is the key to much subsequent German political and economic history, not least, as we shall be seeing, in the second half of the nineteenth century, and the twentieth when Wagner re-stated the problem in the molten music of his opera *Tristan and Isolde.*

It is surely no accident that another great German medieval poet, Wolfram von Eschenbach, in his *Parsifal,* should have tackled the same problem of innocence and experience in the wasteland of human love and death and epitomised his teaching in the one word, *Mitleid,* compassion. Both poets are inviting their readers to feel with and for men and women caught up in the perennial human predicament: as Joseph Campbell has put it in *The Masks of God,*[7] it is the artist's supreme gift to be able to "create these moments of aesthetic arrest". In such moments can often be discovered the essence of a historical situation.

Our third clue in the psycho-history of Germany is Martin Luther and the aftermath of the German Reformation. In his book *Young Man Luther – A Study in Psycho-Analytic History*[8] Erik H. Erikson demonstrates the nature of that one man's identity crisis, his probing question to himself – who am I? In collective terms this was precisely the question of the German princedoms and duchies – who exactly were they? No longer even approximately contained within the fold of the Holy Roman Empire, they were questioning on religious, economic and political grounds the father-figure of pope and emperor in an analogous way to that in which young Martin Luther found it necessary to question the authority of his own personal father and the collective father figure in Rome. However, and this is the paradox, the very violence of that challenge produced a backlash both in subjective psychology and objectively in the sequence of events: Martin Luther himself became the almost tyrannical father-figure, and after having first championed the peasants' cause identified himself with the petty authority figures of the Protestant German princes in their territories, the little fathers of their own territorial particularisms. As Erikson puts it (p.232): "In spite of having reacted more violently than anyone else against indulgences and against usury, Luther helped prepare the metaphysical misalliance between economic self-interest and affiliation so prominent in the Western world."

Without having necessarily to go all the way with Tawney's equation of Protestantism with capitalism, it is important to recognise the reality of that 'metaphysical misalliance', which is nowhere more strikingly seen than in Germany. Basically it was just this that constituted the core issue of the secularised lands and the Thirty Years' War. No wonder Berthold Brecht found it necessary to personify his dramatic protest, as relevant to the twentieth as to the seventeenth-century German scene, in the form of Mother Courage. In psycho-historical terms this may be seen as the dominance of the newly-clothed father-figure in the territorial prince, who is seeking to establish for himself and his people a sense of their own identity, feeling constrained so to do as over against his neighbours. This may be contrasted with the evolution of socio-political life in sixteenth and seventeenth-century Britain and likened to some extent with the French religious wars of the sixteenth century, 'that notable spectacle of our public death' as Montaigne described them. In the case of France it was Henry IV ('Paris is worth a mass') and Louis XIV (*'L'Etat, c'est moi'*), who brought new life to their country at the cost of the curtailment of civil liberties. In the case of Germany, it was Prussia first under the Great Elector and then under Frederick the Great, which performed a similar function.

Such considerations lead on to an understanding of the polarisation of German life between Potsdam and Weimar and, above all, to that uniquely German phenomenon, Goethe's *Faust*. It is our contention that Potsdam symbolised the misconceived attempt to secure German, and indeed at various periods, European integration by imposing the will of the father instead of wooing that integration by a proper and equal valuation of the mother. By so doing there was a misdirected effort to achieve maturity of political, economic and cultural life without paying the price that all such raising of the level of consciousness demands, namely the price of tragedy: the acceptance of the law of human development that integration demands the acceptance of opposites. Tragedy means the acceptance of crucifixion, and Faust by his bargain with Mephistopheles was hoping to win the prize without paying the price. That was why, more than a hundred years later, as we shall be seeing, the raving Nietzsche was to sign one of his last letters, 'The Crucified'.

Meanwhile in eighteenth-century Germany Goethe (1748-1832) was expressing through his own genius this fatal evasiveness of his own people.[9] The dilemma in which he found himself can be compared to that in which Erasmus found himself *vis-à-vis* Lutheranism in the sixteenth century, but in Goethe's case it was *vis-à-vis* the French Revolution and Napoleon. This once again expresses in Goethe's admiration for the latter, in spite of the French threat to the security of the Weimar court, the persistent attempt, an essentially German one, to obtain the fruits of growth without paying for them.

Thomas Mann in his *Last Essays*[10] summed up very well the ambiguous position of Goethe in the psycho-history of Germany: her greatest man who achieved some of the loftiest visions there have ever been of human destiny but who at the same time failed — and here he epitomised the German people — to perceive the nature of the price of growth in collective political consciousness and the need for paying its price.

"The tragedy for the patriots who wished to educate Germany to the ideal of political liberty was that his incontestable greatness lent such weight of authority to his 'obstructing principle'. In Germany greatness tends to a kind of hypertrophy which is itself undemocratic. Between the great man and the common folk in Germany a gulf forms, 'an emotional detachment' to use Nietzsche's favourite phrase. . . ."[11]

Our reading of German psycho-history is that for the reasons already given that gulf had formed itself by the end of the eighteenth century and the beginning of the nineteenth century. The second half of the nineteenth century with Bismarck and the first half of the twentieth century with the failure of the Weimar Republic and the horror of the Nazi régime were to witness further unsuccessful attempts to bridge the gulf.

From Bismarck to Weimar: the Events of 1815 to 1933

For the reasons already set out there was no German nation at the beginning of the nineteenth century, but a huge medley of some 234 territorial states. The effect of the Napoleonic campaigns was such as to provide a decisive impetus to the eventual growth of German nationalism. After the Treaty of Vienna in 1815, when the number of separate German states was reduced to thirty-nine, nationalism and liberalism, particularly the work of Von Humboldt and Hardenberg, the formation of a *Zollverein* or Customs Union and the influence of Fichte's nationalistic ideas, seemed likely to advance in unity. For a variety of reasons however, chief among them the failure of the Frankfurt Parliament of 1848, this had become impossible by the middle of the century, and nationalism and conservatism under the aegis of Prussia became the formative and often disastrous unifying force.

As Barraclough remarks in *The Origins of Modern Germany*,[12] "the fundamental issue at stake was less the struggle for supremacy between Austria and Prussia than that between the principles of unity and particularism. What Prussia set out under Bismarck to overcome in the wars of 1866 and 1870 was the particularism enshrined in the Peace of Vienna; and its blows were directed at Austria and then at France, as the two mainstays of German particularism, the two powers which had organised German territorial disunity in their own interests and to further their own ends. But Prussian policy under Bismarck was designed to further Prussian, not German, interests and to safeguard Prussia's position as a great power; and it was only Bismarck's success that gave general credence to the theory that Prussian self-preservation and the cause of German unity were identical." Summarising Bismarck's victorious policy as evinced in his defeat first of Austria in 1866 and secondly France in 1871, Barraclough writes: "he offered the German people unity but at the expense of radical reform which alone made unity worthwhile." Bismarck's character was, according to Bertrand Russell,[13] "Titanic, complex and divided" and, quoting Naumann, *"Er dachte Europa von Preussen aus,"* "He thought of Europe in terms of Prussia."

When by 1890 economic requirements and Social Democratic political pressures were for diverse reasons demanding some kind of reform, the young Kaiser William II 'dropped the pilot' (Bismarck) in order to preserve the influence of the monarchy and the essentials of the old régime. Chancellor Caprivi's efforts in the early nineties to broaden and increase liberal tendencies were nipped in the bud by conservative political and business interests, themselves reacting to rapid industrialisation and the fact that between 1849 and 1910 the urban population increased from ten million to forty million. Another aspect of this period was the Kaiser's attempt to divert attention from the German domestic scene by striking attitudes in foreign affairs and claiming for Germany a "place in the (colonial) sun". In the context of the overall Great Power Struggle and the division of Europe into two armed camps, marked by the Russo-French Alliance of 1894 in spite of Bismarck's earlier anxiety to prevent just this through the Reinsurance Treaty with Russia which had not been continued, and then the Entente Cordiale between France and Britain in 1904, the Kaiserreich found itself ranged with Italy and Austria in a diplomatic conflict, which was to culminate in Sarajevo and the outbreak of the First World War.

Germany's defeat by the Allies in 1918 led to the disappearance of the monarchy and the establishment of the Weimar Republic. However, just as in the days of Bismarck and the Kaiserreich the Reichstag had been nothing but, in Karl Liebknecht's contemptuous phrase, 'the fig-leaf of absolutism', so now under the first presidency of Ebert the young republic was only enabled to survive and briefly stretch its constitutional wings by means of the good offices of the German army, defeated in a foreign war but destined to play a twofold decisive role in peace, first through the assurances of support against a left-wing extremist putsch, given to Ebert by the German General Gröner from the military scene of defeat and then by General Von Seekt, commander of the army of 100,000 men permitted to Germany by the Allies, who supported the young Social Democratic government threatened from the extreme Right and Left.

"The Reichswehr, Mr President, stands behind me." It was this force under his determined and skilful leadership which was forged into a professional military core throughout the twenties; each highly trained member of it was potential officer material, and its products largely took over the officer positions as soon as regular recruitment became possible after the Allied vigilance was relaxed. "The civil war which raged for the first three months of 1919 sealed the fate of the German Republic."[14] The 'oldest and least modified Reichs-German type was recreated with the insignia of the modern technician.'[15]

It now only remains to relate the series of factors which led to the collapse of the Weimar Republic in 1933. First, there was the fact that, quite simply, the majority of the German people did not believe in it. Secondly, it was constitutionally inept. Thirdly, it was burdened from the outset by reparations, the inflation which wiped out the middle class as an effective body of potential influence, and the War Guilt clause of the Treaty of Versailles. Fourthly, Stresemann's policy of fulfilment came too late. Fifthly, Germany, sharing in a world trend, experienced the full force of the world economic crisis of 1929 accompanied by a vast crisis of unemployed within her own borders. Sixthly, Chancellor Brünning proved too weak to resist either the pressures of the German baron and military caste as exemplified by Von Papen and Schleicher, or the monumental, prestige stupidity of the ancient President Hindenberg. Seventhly, in Germany as elsewhere in Europe the real menace seemed to those in power to be constituted by the Communist Left rather than the Fascist Right. Finally and conclusively, the medicine-man of evil genius, Adolf Hitler, was busy in the wings plotting with his storm-troopers to take centre stage with the Messianic message of total salvation, which had so often before in German history dazed, dazzled and deceived the mass of the German people.

One further phenomenon needs to be mentioned at this stage, namely the German Youth Movement. This originated between 1896 and 1914 as a kind of romantic protest against the 'establishment' of the Kaiserreich and against urbanisation. The personification of this was the Wandervogel, who with his peers, knapsacks on backs, roamed the countryside trying to revive old folk music and dancing, feeling rather pathetically for Germany's roots. Perhaps most Wandervogel were leftish, but their most marked characteristic was 'escape' from the sordid, political scene. In Weimar times the German Youth Movement became fragmented and was eventually drowned in the deluge of the Hitler Youth, though it should in all justice be remembered that some of the most gallant members of the anti-Hitler Resistance movement, Stauffenberg among them, had been Wandervogel in their youth.[16]

The Interpretations of Psycho-History

In his book *The Disinherited Mind* Erich Heller tells the story of Karl Valentin, the metaphysical clown (p.154). Valentin is seen searching for his latchkey in a dark street, illuminated by only one lamp round and round which he is circling in the small circle of light that falls on the pavement.

> Enter a policeman: What have you lost?
> Valentin: The key to my house.
> Policeman: Are you sure you lost it here?
> Valentin: No (pointing to a dark corner), over there!
> Policeman: Then why on earth are you looking for it here?
> Valentin: There is no light over there!

Heller suggests that history, maybe, is the circle of light, but that the key we are looking for is likely to be in a place not illumined by the street lamp. Because that is the conviction which also informs this psycho-history of Germany, we shall now look for our key in the place not illumined by the street lamps of the historian, namely in the minds of a philosopher, a poet and a novelist. By reflecting on some of their utterances we may receive illumination concerning the nature of those determinants of German history between 1815 and 1933, which lie beneath the level of politics and economics.

Both the person and the writings of Friedrich Nietzsche (1844-1900) reveal the underlying forces which determined the events of German history in the nineteenth and twentieth centuries. A man of superb intellect and magnificent depth of vision, his own development was, perhaps perversely, influenced by the mode of his upbringing and by the state of

German and Swiss university education when he took service in it as a teacher. The contradiction between academic sterility and instinctive life he identified with the memorable phrase describing German professors as the 'culture-barbarians'. The split he depicts in his philosophical writings as the conflict between the Apollonian and Dionysian modes of apprehending reality, and his awareness of both, is well illustrated in his relationship with Richard Wagner, first adoring, then condemning. So strong were the sociological and psychological pressures acting on Nietzsche's sensitive spirit that his mind and to some degree his body was literally crucified: hence that famous letter already alluded to, signed 'The Crucified'. He had been torn in pieces by the savage forces fighting over and through him for the possession of Germany. No wonder that later on, not least because of the form in which his work reached the public through the malign channel of his sister, he was claimed by the Nazis as their hero, the prophet and justifier of the anti-Christian Superman. They nailed him to one side of the cross only, the Dionysian one, but Nietzsche's position is in the middle, a pathetic and noble witness to the truth of the middle way, which was to be rejected both by the Kaiserreich and Hitler and misguidedly and ruinously explored by the Weimar Republic. In other words Nietzsche's person and writings demonstrate the price that was to be paid both by the individual and the collective in the cause of individuation. His own book *Ecce Homo* has as its sub-title *How One Becomes What One Is.* Nietzsche realised the fateful and tragic psycho-historical connection between the individual's psychic condition and that of society as a whole when he wrote: "For one thing is needful: that a human being attain his satisfaction with himself. . . . Whoever is dissatisfied with himself is always ready to take revenge; therefore, we others, will be his victims." What a horribly accurate prognostication of the fate of the Jewish victims of Nazi persecution!

"Towards the end of his conscious life (*c.* 1889) Nietzsche was convinced that the culture of Europe was doomed; that an eclipse of all traditional values was at hand, and that modern European man, this pampered child of the optimistically rational eighteenth century, would needs go astray in a wilderness without path or guidance. He quoted Pascal, who said that without the Christian belief we shall become to ourselves what nature and history will become to us — a monster and a chaos. We, he adds, shall make this prophecy come true. The sections of The Will to Power which are concerned with the coming of European nihilism read like a vast elaboration of that dictum of Pascal's as well as of Goethe's prophecy of the prosaic age."[17]

One hundred years later in 1971 George Steiner in *In Bluebeard's Castle* gave a mournful, documented verification of this prophecy.

The human weakness from which Nietzsche suffered and which was to destroy him, and which has itself been the destructive agent at work in German history generally, was spiritual impatience. Just because he experienced keenly the tension between reason and instinct, the world of the father and of the mother, Apollo and Dionysus, because he strove to identify with neither or both, he was broken between them. He had dared the vision of a Faust, but because as a man he could not bear, could not embrace the devil too, he failed in his mission at the time, was crippled by illness and thrown on the human junk-heap, but lived on through his writings to offer an explanatory illumination of a particular phase of German and indeed Western history. The novels of Joseph Conrad offer a superb comment on the predicament of modern man unable or unwilling to transcend this destructive element by immersion in it without drowning.

The German poet, Rilke (1875-1926), provides further guidance in our psycho-historical elucidation. As a young man he himself came strongly under the influence of Nietzsche, and there is a basic similarity in their diagnosis of the sickness of their age. Rilke's 'Angel' figure corresponds to Nietzsche's Apollo, Rilke's Orpheus to Nietzsche's Dionysus. Both addressed themselves at various stages to the problem of power: "We shall come to see Rilke as the St. Francis of the Will to Power", writes Heller[18] and indeed Rilke found himself caught in that role, especially during the First World War when the horror of events strangled his poetic cry. Where he investigated perhaps a rather different aspect of human reality than Nietzsche did, but where he was solidly in the middle of the traditional German dilemma, was his musings on the relationship between love, life and death, his aim being "To presuppose the oneness of life and death". Turning that phrase into love and death or love and illness, there is a direct link between mediaeval Tristan and Isolde's *Liebestod* and the constant theme (as we shall be seeing) of the thought of Thomas Mann.

Meanwhile Nietszche was surely speaking for Rilke when he remarked, "He who no longer finds what is great in God, will find it nowhere — he must either deny it or create it." The Weimar Republic failed to create it, the Nazi *régime* denied it, but Rilke invented it in his poetry, especially in his treatment of death. Heller pays eloquent tribute to both Nietzsche and Rilke in the following passage, which can also serve as a psycho-historical clue: "It is the redeeming achievement of Nietzsche and Rilke that they have raised, the one in the intensely felt plight of his thought, the other in his intensely meditated poetry, the abysmal contradictions of their age to a plane where doubt and confusion once more dissolve into the certainty of mystery."[19]

As a prologue to the consideration of our psycho-historical clue in the work of Thomas Mann, it is worth glancing at a novel written in the 1930s by Odon von Horvath, called *A Child of Our Times*.[20] Its content is aptly described by Franz Werfel (p.VIII) as a 'demonology of the middle class' with the 'middle' man as 'servile' man. It is painful reading, for it describes the incompetence and impotence of the Weimar Republic, robbed by the inflation of its better middle class, so that its inferior or shadow side easily succumbed to the demonology of the Nazi programme. In an Appreciation introducing this book, Stefan Zweig writes: "And these novels, bearing the stamp of true poetry and masterpieces of their kind, form one of the most important German documents of the age."

It is neither our intention nor our need to present a potted biography of Thomas Mann. What is required is a careful look at the main phases of his life in so far as they evoked from him attitudes towards or utterances about German history, whether distant or contemporary. Born in 1875 of well-to-do Lübeck merchant stock, his father a senator of the city and his mother of Portuguese Latin American extraction, Thomas

Mann grew up in comfortable circumstances and in confor-
mity with the social mores of the day. After the death of his
father, the family moved to Munich, where he attended the
university, frequented cultural circles and began writing.
Buddenbrooks appeared in 1901 and is of interest to us
because in it the author handles two of his most persistent
themes, the sick role of the artist in society, Hanno
Buddenbrook *malgré lui,* and the decline of a powerful
bourgeoisie, caught between a vanishing Kaiserreich and a
beckoning or threatening democratic socialism.

The outbreak of the First World War in 1914 precipitated
the following reflection from this no longer young man: "My
chief feeling is a tremendous curiosity — and, I admit it, the
deepest sympathy for this execrated fateful Germany, which,
if she has hitherto not unqualifiedly held 'civilisation' as the
highest good, is at any rate preparing to smash the most
despicable police state in the world."[21] (p.70). This rather
strange remark came from him within the German front as a
non-combatant, exempt from military service on health
grounds. Which did he mean by the "despicable police state",
France or Russia? On 11 January 1915 his position became
clearer: "For after all, these things must be acknowledged as
history on the grand scale, although a certain radical, intellectual, humanitarian-pacifist group represents the war pretty
much as a swindle." (p.74) In this case there is no doubt to
what he is referring: his brother, Heinrich and his associates
of the small but vocal anti-war group in Germany. During the
war years Thomas Mann occupied himself with writing a life
of Frederick the Great and his *Reflections of a Non-Political
Man.* Both of these must have prompted him to such a
reflection as the following:

"I have long believed that it is impossible, for internal more
than external reasons, to create an authentic political life in
Germany. . . . It all comes from the fact that we are not a
nation. Rather, we are something like the quintessence of
Europe, so that we are subject to the clash of Europe's
spiritual contradictions without having a national synthesis.
There is no German solidarity and ultimate unity. European
wars will no longer be waged on German soil, you say? Oh
yes, they will be. There will always be German civil war in
fact." (p.82)

It is illuminating historically to lay this alongside Hebbel's comment of December 1843: "We Germans, unlike the English and French, cannot look upon ourselves as an organic continuation of the past; for that which, after all, we must call our history is more in the nature of a case-history." If that is German history, perhaps all history is best regarded as a case — or psycho-history: the story of Amfortas' wound (see Chapter VI). Some decades after Hebbel, Nietzsche remarked of Wagner's music: "This kind of music expresses best what I think of the Germans; they are of the day before yesterday and the day after tomorrow. Today has not yet come."

These early remarks of Thomas Mann are pregnant and prophetic: they begin to explain what Erich Heller in his own brilliant study of *Mann, The Ironic German*[22] has described as his 'conservative imagination'. In this connection it is particularly interesting to compare Mann's treatment of Frederick the Great, sympathetic but not uncritical of that *'böse Mensch'* as the Empress Maria Theresa called him, with his own remark some thirty years later in 1939 when already in exile from Nazi Germany, "Absolute politics is the end of freedom." In the preface to *Reflections of a Non-Political Man* Mann says of himself and this book: "not a work of art, but the work of an artist whose existence was shaken to its foundations, whose self-respect was brought into question, and whose troubled condition was such that he was completely unable to produce anything else" (a striking resemblance to Rilke's reaction at the same time). Mann described this work of 1918 as "a last great rearguard action of romantic middle-class mentality in the face of advancing 'modernity', an action conducted not without gallantry". In his study of Mann Heller comments: "At the troubled heart of Reflections of a Non-Political Man is a religious imagination and religious conscience in conflict with a sceptical mind — the deepest source of Thomas Mann's irony." (p.146)

This poses the question: is irony an adequate philosophical basis for living? Kierkegaard thought not, and Mann, the artist, whose chief merit as a creator of fiction was his irony, was driven by events in his own life experience to transcend irony.

In 1919 Mann writing in Munich remarks, still with some complacency, of the murder of Kurt Eisner and the attempted left-wing putsch: "Well, then, it was wild, but we are well and have passed through all the storms unaffected." (pp.94-5). If the Mann household could be unaffected, how easy for the bulk of Germans to remain 'unaffected' by the storms of political life which were even then hastening the country's ruin! In a few years' time the average decent German was to deny knowledge of the concentration camps! However Mann continued indignantly, "Not a word about the Entente's peace. The blindness of the victors is revealed — whom the gods will destroy — the venomous old man who concocts this peace in the insomniac nights of old age has slant eyes. Perhaps he has a blood right to dig the grave of Western culture and bring on Kirghisdan." Such a doubtful specu-lation reveals Mann's ironic awareness that Western democ-racy in the hands of Clemenceau might be digging its own grave, itself a process made necessary by the aggressive forces pressing from the East. The note of indignation continues to be struck:

"What was Canossa compared to the spectacle the German Emperor will present before the tribunal of the Entente? Perhaps it won't come to that (it did not of course), but the possibility is enough to make it a reality for us. . . . Our entire national existence to be condemned as guilty and erroneous, that is what my Betrachtungen would not concede, long before people imagined that we might ever come to such a pass. That the great tradition of Germanism from Luther to Bismarck and Nietzsche should be refuted and discredited — this is the fact which is HAILED by many among us, the fact which is laid down in many a carefully considering paragraph of the peace conditions, and the fact which I was opposing in my fight against the 'civilisation literatus'."

The not so very many in Germany who hailed that fact were the Weimar Social Democrats and intelligentsia, of whom brother Heinrich was a leading representative; the many in the former Allied camp hoped by means of the Versailles clauses to muzzle the German tiger. Later in the same letter Mann extends his analysis of the 1919 scene:

"It lay in the nature of things that my opponents would triumph; I recognised that early and said as much. One must take a contemplative, even a resignedly cheerful view, read Spengler and understand that the victory of England and America seals and completes the civilising, rationalising pragmatisms of the West which is the fate of every aging culture. More and more I see this war (in so far as it was not social revolution from the start — that is the other side of the matter —) as a vast quixotism, a last mighty effort to rear up and strike a blow on behalf of the German Middle Ages, which remained astoundingly well-preserved before collapsing with a rattle of bones. What's coming now is Anglo-Saxon domination of the world, that is perfected civilisation."

Leaving aside the deep and not altogether correct, ironical thrust of the last sentence, it makes odd reading but sound diagnosis, for it was precisely medieval particularism and local absolutism, inadequately transposed after 1870 into the Kaiserreich and fearing despairingly the 'modernity' menace of democracy, which precipitated Germany into war. On top of the medieval layer of psycho-historical causation lay the extravagance of Cervantes: quixotism as the early, relatively civilised rehearsal of the storm-trooper.

In a letter to Keyserling of 18 January 1920 Mann writes (p.101):

"I was very much interested in your remark that before too long the Conservatives will again have the greatest say in Germany. I too believe that: in the end nature restores the balance somehow, and 'the German is conservative'. Wagner will prove to have been for ever right in that regard. For this reason nothing is more important than the infusion of intelligence into German conservatism — and all your activity, after all, comes down to that in the end. For what is at stake is nothing other than the celebrated 'reunion of intellect and soul'."

It was because intelligence was not infused into German conservatism that the lunacy of the extreme Right triumphed under Hitler over the politically impotent intelligence of Weimar. It is moving to observe Mann's personal struggle to understand this and to adapt himself:—

On 5 December 1922 he writes (p.120):

"Thus I was affirming the revolution . . . I dated the Republic not from 1918 but from 1914. It came into being in the hearts of the youth at that time, as they faced death on the field of honour. In saying this I contributed something toward a definition of the Republic I mean — I certainly did not hail the Republic until I said what I meant by it. How do I define it? Approximately as the opposite of what exists today. But for that very reason, the attempt to infuse something like an idea, a soul, a vital spirit into this grievous state without citizens seemed to me no mean undertaking."

Earlier that year he had issued his essay, 'On a German Republic: Call to Youth to Support Weimar'. The following extract from a letter about the Ruhr makes abundantly clear just how difficult, if not impossible, that call was to prove for patriotic young Germans of the twenties, who could neither be convinced or convince others that their Weimar politicians could stand up to illegitimate foreign and domestic pressures put upon them:

"Our Frenchmen are behaving brilliantly. They seem determined to give the lie to everyone in Germany who urges moderation. One hears that the details about the Ruhr are not exaggerated but rather lag behind the truth. The anger is terrible — deeper and more united than that which brought on Napoleon's fall. There is no predicting the outcome. And the unfortunate part of it is that a French retreat, desirable though that would be, would signify the triumph of nationalism in domestic politics. Must the better side of Germany really be forced into this dilemma? Germany was completely malleable in 1918, but the others, who were convinced that they were so much better, have shown little capacity to learn." (7 February 1923, p.122)

Mann perceived with devastating irony and exactitude the terrible significance of Hindenburg's elevation!

"The candidacy of Hindenburg is 'Linden Tree' — to put it mildly. An article of mine in the *Neue Freie Presse* denounces this shameful exploitation of the German people's romantic impulses. In it I say that I 'shall be proud of our nation's political discipline and instinct for life and for the future if on Sunday it refrains from electing an antediluvian valiant as its chief of state." (23 April 1925, p.144)

On 15 May 1933 Mann wrote:

"And it is my deepest conviction that this whole 'German Revolution' is indeed wrong and evil. It lacks all the characteristics which have won the sympathy of the world for genuine revolutions, however bloody they may have been. In its essence it is not a 'rising', no matter how its proponents rant on, but a terrible fall into hatred, vengeance, lust for killing, and petty bourgeois mean-spiritedness. I shall never believe that any good can come out of it for either Germany or the world."

By chance Mann managed to evade the Nazi tentacles by remaining in Switzerland in 1933 where he had travelled in the course of a lecture tour. From there he records his mounting horror: "But I cannot say how much I have been affected by the atrocities of 20 June, the Austrian horrors, and then the coup d'etat of that creature, his further elevation, which undoubtedly represents a new consolidation of his tottering regime." (4 August 1934, p.224) (These are references to the Röhm purge, Dolfuss' murder and Hitler's presidency.) In addition to an 'Open Letter' of remonstrance to the German people he wrote: "So-called National Socialism has no place at all within any European and ethical framework. It stands in opposition not only to 'liberalism' and 'Western Democracy', but also to civilisation in general – using that word in a sense that not even German KULTUR mysticism can ignore." (3 September 1934, p.226)

In 1938 developments in Germany and Europe had driven Mann into exile in the USA, where eventually he took American citizenship. In another letter (December 1938, p.290) he summarised the sad fate of Germany under the Weimar régime:

"Mistakes were made, of omission and commission: that we cannot deny. The spiritual leaders of the Republic did not err, perhaps, on the side of the spirit; but they did so in the matter of leadership and the consciousness of their responsibility. Freedom was sometimes compromised; often it was not treated with the care and concern which the circumstances in Germany demanded. But was that to be wondered at? Freedom is a more complex and delicate thing than force. It is not so simple to live under as force. And we German intellectuals were politically very young and inexperienced . . ."

He broadcast to the German people from the USA in 1941:

"But there is one thing which has been done really for your sake, which has developed from social and not private conscience. With every day I am more and more certain that the time will come, and in fact is already near at hand, when you will thank me for it and rate it higher than my stories and books. And this is, that I warned you, when it was not yet too late, against the depraved powers under whose yoke you are harnessed to-day and who lead you through innumerable misdeeds to incredible misery."

In a letter to Walter von Molo (7 September 1945, p.483) he touches on a fundamental idea: "I gave a brief account of the development of German *Innerlichkeit.* I rejected the theory of the two Germanys, one good and one evil. The evil Germany, I said, is the good Germany gone wrong — the good one caught up in misfortune, guilt and doom."

Mann made return visits to Germany after the Second World War, trying to do what he could to hold East and West Germany together in some kind of dialogue. As an artist and citizen he had lived through three years of his own country's evolution, as a young man in the Kaiserreich, as a distinguished novelist in the Weimar Republic, absenting himself but with increasing difficulty from the political scene, as a refugee from Nazi oppression and outspoken critic of Hitlerism, to a final stage of attempted but ineffectual conciliation between the two halves of his divided postwar nation. He died in 1955.

Because the deeper aspects of Mann's life as a citizen are available in the works of fiction he created and because, as we have seen from this short introduction, he worked in fearfully acute consciousness of his historical context, *The Magic Mountain*[23] provides splendid source material for the psycho-historian.

This novel was published in 1924, but he had been working on it since 1915, and in his own foreword to it he takes his readers fully into his confidence.

"This story we say belongs to the long ago; is already, so to speak, covered with historic mould, and unquestionably to be presented in the tense best suited to a narrative out of the depths of the past. . . . The exaggerated pastness of our narrative is due to its taking place before the epoch when a certain crisis shattered its way through life and consciousness and left a deep chasm behind. It takes place — or rather, deliberately to avoid the present tense, it took place and had taken place — in the long ago, in the old days, the days of the world before the Great War, in the beginning of which so much began that has scarcely yet left off beginning. Yes, it took place before that; yet not so long before. Is not the pastness of the past the profounder, the completer, the more legendary, the more immediately before the present it falls? More than that, our story has, of its own nature, something of the legend about it now and again." (p.XI)

Here in a few words Mann has established the dimension of psycho-history, constituted of a specific time and place, Europe before 1914, and also of the long ago, once upon a time, mythological time. The 'certain crisis' and 'deep chasm' have certainly not even yet, sixty years later, 'left off beginning'; that past is our present. Finally the author throws out the suggestion that the recent past, such as the one with which he is concerned, is particularly profound because we are more recently severed from it than from remoter epochs in the same way that nothing is more remote from a young adolescent than his own immediate childhood. We have to grow old to come to terms with our youth: we have to advance into the future if we would redeem the past.

When Mann is introducing us to his hero, young Hans Castorp, he writes (p.32):

"A man lives not only his personal life, as an individual, but also, consciously or unconsciously, the life of his epoch and his contemporaries. He may regard the general, impersonal foundations of his existence as definitely settled and taken for granted, and be as far from assuming a critical attitude toward them as our good Hans Castorp really was: yet it is quite conceivable that he may none the less be vaguely conscious of the deficiencies of his epoch and find them prejudicial to his own moral well-being.''

Those last few words describe admirably the average 'decent chap', not only of Germany but of Europe as a whole, afloat in the turbulent flood of pre-1914 history.

"In an age that affords no satisfying answer to the eternal question of 'why? to what end?', a man who is capable of achievement over and above the average and expected modicum must be equipped either with a moral remoteness and single-mindedness which is rare indeed and of heroic mould, or else with an exceptional robust vitality." The type of character these words evoke is wonderfully portrayed in Ulrich, the hero of Musil's *The Man Without Qualities,* which was being written at much the same time in another part of Europe. Both Hans Castorp from Bremen and Ulrich from Vienna were posing the problem of their age, which both authors after the First World War suggested had to be solved by war because no other solution to the impasse of their lives had been discovered: a psycho-historical cause for 1914 and 1939, perceived in the middle of the 1920s. In *The Magic Mountain* Mann puts these words into the mouth of Naphta (pp.400 ff.):

"I was already tolerably well aware that what is called liberalism-individualism, the humanistic conception of citizenship — was the product of the Renaissance, but the fact leaves me entirely cold, realising as I do, that your great heroic age is a thing of the past, its ideals defunct, or at least lying at their latest gasp, while the feet of those who will deal them the *coup de grâce* are already before the door."

Indeed they were; both Mann and Musil have many similar prophetic passages about the advent of the 'dare-men', the rule of the jackboot.

Let us attend to the ominous totalitarian thunder in the following words of dire prognostication:

"In the past five hundred years the principle of freedom has outlived its usefulness. An educational system which still conceives of itself as a child of the enlightenment, with criticism as its chosen medium of instruction, the liberation and cult of the ego (in fact the very essence of Weimar), the solvent of forms of life which are absolutely fixed — such a system may still, for a time, reap an empty rhetorical advantage; but its reactionary character is, to the initiated, clear beyond any doubt. All educational organisations worthy of the name have always recognised what must be the ultimate and significant principle of pedagogy: namely the absolute mandate, the iron bond, discipline, sacrifice, the renunciation of the ego, the curbing of the personality. And lastly, it is an unloving miscomprehension of youth to believe that it finds its pleasure in freedom: its deepest pleasure lies in obedience."

What an exact recipe for the Hitler Youth or the Young Pioneers: *'Gehorsam'*, whether of the Right or the Left!

"No," Naphta went on, "Liberation and development of the individual are not the key to our age, they are not what our age demands: What it needs, what it wrestles after, what it will create is Terror."

So that, according to Mann's artistic vision, was what people were really after in the 1920s: they got what they desired in the 1930s.

The Hitler Phenomenon: the Events of a Dozen Years (1933-1945)

The National-Socialist régime and Germany's role in the Second World War can be traced back to the confluence of two forces, one political and collective, the other individual: the former was the plight of the Weimar Republic in 1929; the latter was the personality of Adolf Hitler. In his massive study, *The German Dictatorship: the Origins, Structure and Consequences of National Socialism*[24] K. D. Bracher provides a useful summary of the defects of the Weimar Republic, which, caught in the conflict between the authoritarian tradition and the new democracy, suffered the following consequences of that conflict. There was firstly, a non-functioning of parliamentary government; secondly, agitation for a presidential system to serve as a kind of ersatz empire or quasi-dictatorship; thirdly, a splintering and lack of co-operation of ideological and politically rigid parties; fourthly, the unchecked rise of anti-democratic movements; fifthly, the militarisation of non-governmental sectors by military groups; sixthly, the spread of a terrorist power philosophy; seventhly, the radicalisation of economically and socially threatened urban and rural middle classes, eighthly the susceptibility of the bureaucracy and the judiciary to ideas of hierarchy, and lastly, the ambiguous role of the army.

In the light of that kind of analysis Hitler's emergence on to the stage of German politics begins to make sense. Himself the son of a minor but quite well-to-do Austrian Customs official, Adolf Hitler was born in 1889 and grew up as a failed artist, performing odd jobs in Vienna to where he had gravitated, but still in touch with his petty bourgeois origin, though there were periods when he was really destitute and down-and-out. On the outbreak of the First World War in 1914 he volunteered for service with a Bavarian regiment, rose to the rank of corporal and was decorated for bravery in the field. After demobilisation the postwar political scene in Munich was to present him with opportunities: that city had experienced briefly Marxist Republican rule under Kurt Eisner but then became a hot-bed of right-wing agitation. Some army officers of this persuasion assigned to Hitler the task of investigating the activities of a group called the German Workers' Party, originally founded by a nationalist blacksmith named Anton Drexler. In April 1920 it changed its name to the National Socialist German Workers' Party, and Hitler became one of its leading members. In the course of 1921 he obtained support from two ladies, Frau Helene Bechstein and Frau Gertrud von Seidlitz and also the approving interest of such men as Goering, Hess and Rosenberg. It is curious that an even earlier member of that party had been Ernst Röhm, who commanded the allegiance of a number of ex-service officers and men and the potential support of ex-Field-Marshal Ludendorff.

When in the summer of 1923 Stresemann initiated his policy of fulfilment by announcing the end of resistance to the French in the Ruhr, a Berlin attempt to establish a military dictatorship failed. Hitler's putsch in Munich proved abortive: after an initial success in the beer cellar when he arrested the leaders of a Bavarian faction, he and his chief backer, Ludendorff, were apprehended by the legitimate government. In April 1924 Hitler was sentenced to five years' imprisonment for attempting to alter the German constitution by force. However he only served nine months, and was then released by sympathetic influences in governing circles. It is important to note that in his court plea Hitler proclaimed: "I believe that the hour will come when the masses, who to-day stand in the streets with our swastika banner will unite with those who fired on them." This was an accurate prophecy of what in fact happened ten years later. While in prison he wrote *Mein Kampf,* where he set down plainly what his programme would be when he came to power. In 1925 membership of the Nazi party stood at 27,000; in 1928 it stood at 108,000, and there had come into existence Hitler's élite corps, the SS (*Schutz-Staffel*). In 1926 he had obtained the support of Dr Goebbels, the future notorious Minister of Propaganda.

As late as May 1928 in the elections the Nazis only won twelve seats in the Reichstag, but, due to the fierce internecine strife of the political parties, not least over the Young Plan, and to the mounting menace of unemployment, the gathering crisis gave Hitler his chance. First, he entered into alliance with the interests of big business in the persons of Hugenberg and Thyssen. Then he and his disciplined followers permeated the whole country, promising a solution to the problems of unemployment, civil insecurity and ill-treatment by foreign powers. In September 1930 with 107 seats the Nazis became the second largest party, and Germany slipped into minority government under Brünning, authorised and enforced by President Hindenburg's invovation of the Emergency Decrees Article No. 48 of the constitution. At the Presidential election in 1932 Hindenburg retained office with 19·4 million votes, but Hitler polled 13·4 million. After a few last months of feverish government by unscrupulous military and aristocratic figures such as Von Scheicher and Von Papen, another election was held. Although this time the Nazi vote was doubled (July 1932), the Nazis still held no absolute majority. In November 1932 they lost two million votes and 34 seats and it seemed as if the old right-wing parties might be winning back their strength. However, a bad winter, constant clashes in the streets between rival armed factions, chiefly Communist and Nazi, the glaring incompetence of the barons' government and the ceaseless, giant-scale propaganda of the Nazis brought first a local voting success in the province of Lippe and then a sweep to power. On 30 January 1933 President Hindenburg invited Hitler to become Chancellor even though his party did not even yet command majority support.

The outstanding events of the next six years can be summarised as follows: February 1933, the Reichstag Fire, the exploitation of that dubious phenomenon by Hitler to get through the Enabling Act and all that came to be associated with *Gleichschaltung,* namely the total subordination of all activities in the state of Nazi control. "The victory of National Socialism, the alarmingly rapid march of an apparently irrevocable totalitarian system of government in Germany, was consolidated in less than two years, between 30 January 1933 and August 1934."[25] Then there was the Night of the Long Knives in June 1934 when Röhm and his henchmen were liquidated, which meant that the Party lost its radical, however brutal, components. A striking degree of economic recovery ensued, the bulldozing of any resistance from the Churches, for instance, Pastor Niemoller's efforts, the start of concentration camps for those not supporting the régime, and a series of successes in foreign policy. Finally came the unopposed reoccupation of the Rhineland in 1936, the overrunning of Austria in 1938 and the bullying of Czechoslovakia, the Munich Agreement, followed by the German-Soviet Pact of 1939 and the outbreak of war with the German invasion of Poland on 3 September 1939.

There followed six years of triumph and disaster for the Germans in the Second World War, on two aspects of which it is of interest to dwell. One is the strange flight of Rudolf Hess, Deputy Leader, on a self-directed peace mission to Britain in 1941. *Motive for a Mission, the Story Behind Hess's Flight to Britain* by James Douglas-Hamilton[26] gives a fascinating picture of the influences, not least those of the Haushofers, father and son, which triggered off this strange lone venture. "And if, my Father," wrote Hess in a letter to Hitler, "this project ends in failure, simply say I was crazy." The story is recorded of Churchill's amazed reaction to the news of Hess's arrival on British soil: "Do you mean to tell me that the Deputy Führer of Germany is in our hands? Well,

Hess or no Hess, I am going to see the Marx brothers!" This
magnificently offhand dismissal of the event proved historically strangely correct: Hess's flight made very little, if any,
difference to the course of events.

The other aspect of the war years which merits consideration is the career of Albert Speer (born 1905), Hitler's
architect, who became his Minister of Armaments and
Munitions, and who ended up as a war criminal in the dock at
Nuremberg and served a prison sentence of twenty years
from 1946 to 1966 in Spandau. His book, *Inside the Third
Reich,* reveals in Speer a man of great gifts, soaring ambition,
crass political blindness, an infatuation for Hitler and at the
last, as he pondered the whole horrific enterprise in which he
had played such a major part, deep contrition. In the
Observer of 9 April 1944 there appeared the following
comment: "Speer is, in a sense, more important for Germany
today than Hitler, Himmler, Goering or the generals. They all
have, in a way, become the mere auxiliaries of the man who
actually directs the giant power machine, charged with
drawing from it the maximum effort under maximum strain.
In him is the very epitome of 'the managerial revolution'."
The events of those dozen black years of German history
could hardly be more appropriately summed up than in the
words of self-condemnation written by Speer of the Nuremberg proceedings: "The trial is necessary. There is a shared
responsibility for such horrible crimes even in an authoritarian state."[27]

The Interpretations of Psycho-history
"Why did humanistic tradition and models of conduct prove
so fragile a barrier against political bestiality? In fact were
they a barrier, or is it more realistic to perceive in humanistic
culture express solicitations of authoritarian rape and
cruelty?"[28]
Unless we can begin to suggest some kind of answer in
historical and psychological terms to this searing question, we
may as well confess bankruptcy of soul and intellect.

A 'mixture of Prussian authoritarianism and Austrian-
Volkisch political and expansionist ideologies' is Bracher's
description of the Hitler régime.[29] Let us apply a psycho-
historical probe to it, for Bracher himself refers to the

'multi-causal nature of historical processes'. Let us begin by pursuing a Wagnerian clue. Wagner (1813-83) was himself a figure not aloof from politics: his revolutionary activities in Dresden in 1849 forced him to take flight to Switzerland, where he remained until 1858. Nor was he anything but deeply involved in the human passion of love. Mathilde Wesendonck and Cosima von Bulow nourished his muse, and we should therefore not be surprised that this genius expressed in his music the deepest longings of the human spirit, both collective and individual. "What the *Ring* says could have been said at any moment in the history of the human race, and it could have been said in any medium: but it so happened that it was said musically in nineteenth-century Germany by a bad-tempered old gentleman in a quilted dressing-gown, named Richard Wagner . . ."[30]

In his own essay 'Opera and the Drama' (1851) Wagner defines the function of the artist as being "to bring the unconscious part of human nature into consciousness within society". This is a perfectly precise description of the *Ring*, for in that tremendous four-part music-drama Wagner reveals through the situations and characters of mythology the underlying impulses in the depth psychology of German society in the second half of the nineteenth century; he depicts the primitive erupting into the sophisticated, he demonstrates the deadly accuracy of Nietzsche's arraignment of the 'culture-barbarians' of the academic life.

Bernard Shaw in *The Perfect Wagnerite* was the earliest to recognise and point to a significance underlying Wagner's treatment of the Nibelung Lied: he gave to it an economic meaning, the clash of the capitalist gods with the socialist gnomes of the underworld. Without denying some legitimacy in this interpretation, we can gain far greater insight by following the guidance of Robert Donington in his book, *Wagner's Ring and its Symbols, the Music and the Myth.*[31] He describes the *Ring* as Wagner's personal and artistic individuation process, that is, how he came to terms with the whole of himself, how the dramatic personae are the aspects of his own personality seeking synthesis and finding it in musical creation. Because that solution of the problem was not available to the German people as a whole, the uprush of the archaic forces, no longer capable of being contained by the outside political and economic institutions of nineteenth and twentieth-century German society, resulted in the daemonic outbreak of Hitlerism and the abomination of the concentration camps.

It is worthwhile reminding ourselves at this point of Wagner's rendering of the plot, bearing in mind that the resonances of its theme vibrated in German hearts with the same kind of spell that Hamlet vibrates in ours or the drum-taps of native music in the hearts of African listeners.

Das Rheingold

Hidden at the bottom of the Rhine lay a mass of magic golden treasure, the possession of which conferred limitless power on whoever gained it, but only at the price of his forswearing love. The three Rhine-maidens, who guarded it, were one day teasing ugly Alberich, the dwarf who coveted the gold. Caught off guard, they lost it to the greedy dwarf, who carried it off to his lair in the underworld. Meanwhile, up above, two giants, Fasolt and Fafner, had built the beautiful castle of Valhalla as an abode for the gods on condition that when they had completed it they should receive as their reward Freia, the Goddess of Love. Wotan, King of the Gods, refused to carry out his side of the bargain, so instead the giants were bribed to accept the magic horde of gold, which Wotan and Loki would have to wrest from Alberich. They made their way to Nibelungenheim, the underground abode of Alberich and his minions. Here Alberich had ordered his brother, Mime, the smith, to forge him out of the gold a cap of invisibility and a ring, the wearer of which would have power over men and gods alike. Alberich, in order to impress his two visitors, changed himself into a dragon, but then the wily God of Fire, Loki, persuaded him to give a further demonstration of his powers by taking on the form of a toad. No sooner had Alberich done so, than Wotan quickly placed his foot on the toad and refused to release him until the wretched toad-Alberich had agreed to surrender cap, ring and all the gold. With a curse on anyone who in future should wear the ring, the dwarf was forced to agree. Returning triumphantly to Valhalla, Wotan and Loki displayed the gold to the two giants, who, releasing their captive, the Goddess

Freia, proceeded to quarrel between themselves about fair shares: in the ensuing fight Fasolt was killed by Fafner, the first instalment of the curse had been paid, and Fafner carried off his booty. The Gods crossed happily over a rainbow bridge into Valhalla, and in the distance could be heard the lamenting cry of the Rhine-maidens.

Die Walküre

Wotan, uneasy about the course of events, which derived from his original deceit over the bargain with the giants, brought into being a band of warrior-maidens, the Valkyries, whose duty it was to convey to Valhalla the bravest warriors slain in battle, where they would be restored to life and constitute a mighty race capable of defending Valhalla against all its enemies. On earth Wotan had begotten two children, Siegmund and Sieglinde, who grew up in ignorance of one another. In a forest lived Hunding, whom Sieglinde had married against her will, but she had been promised aid and protection by a mysterious stranger, who had driven his sword up to the hilt into the trunk of the tree which supported the roof of the hut of Hunding and who had promised that one day a protector would arrive and identify himself by being able to draw out the sword. Sure enough, one wild, stormy night, when Hunding was out hunting, an exhausted man staggered across the threshold seeking succour. This was Siegmund, with whom Sieglinde fell in love. Her husband, returning, vowed that after one night's guest hospitality, he would challenge Siegmund to combat, but Sieglinde gave Hunding a sleeping potion, the two discovered their affinity, Siegmund triumphantly drew out the sword, and they both fled away into the forest.

Now although this was part of Wotan's design — he had been the mysterious stranger — his wife, Fricka, scandalised by the breaking of marriage vows, demanded that the two lovers should be punished. Wotan reluctantly ordered his favourite Valkyrie, Brunhilde, to deliver over Siegmund to Hunding. She encountered Siegmund, hotly pursued by Hunding, but was so moved by his plight and her own instinctive awareness that Wotan did not really desire Siegmund's death, that she protected him in the ensuing fight. Then Wotan himself came on the scene and shattered

Siegmund's sword with his own spear with the result that he died at Hunding's hands, whom however Wotan then slew. Brunhilde, afraid of Wotan's wrath, gathered up Sieglinde and bore her away into hiding. In face of this defiance, more in sorrow than in anger, Wotan decided that Brunhilde must be punished for her disobedience: hastily she arranged for Sieglinde's welfare while awaiting the birth of a son who was to be a great hero and placed in her charge the broken pieces of Siegmund's sword. As her punishment Brunhilde was banished from Valhalla and placed to sleep on a mountain top, surrounded by flames, through which only a hero could ever penetrate, and he who did so would be a worthy husband for her.

Siegfried

Twenty years later, after Sieglinde's death at the birth of her son, Siegfried, the boy, was being brought up by Mime, who taught him his blacksmith's craft. As soon as he was grown up, Siegfried demanded of Mime that he should forge him a sword from the fragments bequeathed to him by his mother, but dissatisfied with Mime's efforts, he finally succeeded in forging it himself into a magnificent weapon, called Nothung or Help-in-need. Meanwhile through all the years the horde of gold had been guarded in a cave by the fearful Fafner in the shape of a dragon. Mime told Siegfried about this beast, but instead of frightening him, he merely stimulated him to attack the monster. He slew Fafner, and a drop of the dragon's blood touched his tongue, which magically enabled him to understand the song of a bird warning him that Mime was trying to poison him and telling him of the magic qualities of the ring. Siegfried put this on, killed Mime and, guided by the bird, went in search of further adventures, which led him eventually to the neighbourhood of the mountain on the summit of which slept Brunhilde. Warned by the Earth spirit, Erda, Wotan had a premonition that the days of the gods were numbered, and that their rule was to be challenged by a heroic human adversary. He tried to stop Siegfried's journey up the mountain side, but Siegfried shattered his spear, and he was forced to retire. The hero burst through the flames unscathed and awakened Brunhilde, who, discovering his identity, renounced her immortal qualities. The two then plighted their troth in an ecstasy of love.

Götterdämmerung, The Twilight of the Gods

After a while Siegfried determined to set off on fresh adventures, leaving Brunhilde with the ring to wear during his absence but taking with him the cap of invisibility, the sword and Brunhilde's horse. One day he arrived at the court of King Gunther, where one of the courtiers was Hagen, the wicked son of Alberich. He knew of Siegfried's deeds and plotted against him. First, he brewed the hero a drink, which caused him to forget his past including the memory of Brunhilde. So Siegfried asked Gunther for the hand in marriage of his sister, Gutrune. Gunther agreed on condition that Siegfried would first help him obtain Brunhilde as his bride. By means of the cap of invisibility Siegfried assumed the form of Gunther, and in spite of Brunhilde's proud resistance, wrested the ring from her finger and compelled her to return to Gunther's court. There the king publicly proclaimed Brunhilde as his queen and gave Gutrune's hand to Siegfried. Naturally when she beheld him Brunhilde upbraided Siegfried with his treachery, but still under the influence of the drink, he paid small attention to her. Full of bitter wrath, Brunhilde then plotted with Hagen to slay Siegfried, the latter thus hoping himself to gain possession of the ring. They hoodwinked Gunther into believing that Siegfried had been unfaithful in respect to Brunhilde and so obtained his consent to the planned assassination. Out on a hunting expedition on the banks of the Rhine, Siegfried was confronted by the Rhine-maidens rising up from the river and beseeching him to restore the ring to them, for otherwise he would surely die. Siegfried paid no heed to the warning; he was joined by Gunther, Hagen and their followers, the effects of the potion began to wear off, and as he was reminiscing about his previous adventures and came to the meeting with Brunhilde, he broke off in his narrative confused, glanced up at a flight of ravens overhead and in that very second was stabbed in the back by Hagen. In the moment of death Siegfried's memory cleared, and he recognised his former love, Brunhilde: Gunther and Hagen both tried to drag the ring off his finger, and in the ensuing fight Gunther was

killed. Brunhilde, at last understanding the whole tragic
sequence of events, ordered a funeral pyre to be erected with
Siegfried's body on it: she laid herself by his side, and the
two were consumed by the leaping flames. The river Rhine
overflowed its banks, engulfing all including Hagen, who had
again tried to sieze the ring. So finally that cursed emblem
was restored to its rightful owners, and a great blaze broke
out across the heavens, signalling the destruction of Valhalla
and the end of the reign of the Gods over man.

As Donington remarks (p.39), "Unconscious experiences,
like eternity, are timeless in just such a sense as the prelude
to 'Rhinegold' the opera suggests." Those opening bars lead
us into the very dimension of the psycho-historical; we know
we are confronted with some timeless element in the German
human experience and indeed of the human experience as a
whole: we twentieth-century 'citizens of megalopolis' have
Rhine-maidens and Valkyries, gods and dwarfs, as well as
heroes, heroines and villains in our hearts. Wagner in a letter
of 1854 pointed out that the *Ring* is best taken as an image
of the self in process of realisation:

"Wotan," he says, "rises to the tragic dignity of willing his
own (ego) destruction. The Ring is a symbol of the Self."
Siegmund, urges Donington, had to fail because he was only
an aspect and not a sufficiently strong one, of Wotan
himself. It is only when *Götterdämmerung* is reached, the
twilight of the gods, that the ultimate meaning of the whole
gigantic drama becomes clear. The twilight of the gods is the
twilight of the ego: either it will transcend itself or be
consumed by its pretensions. The superman must become the
integrated man or he will revert to the role of the 'blond
beast'.

Bernard Levin in the article already quoted can help us yet
one stage further:

"It is Wotan who supplies the clue: the tragedy after all is
precipitated by his making a promise that he cannot keep,
and then breaking it, which is mankind's story in a nutshell.
Wotan is, perhaps, the greatest single figure in all art, and if
he is, it is because of his limitless complexity. It is he who
makes the point that he and his great enemy the Nibelungs
are two sides of the same coin (Lichtalberich and

Schwarzalberich): in a sense the whole work is the story of Wotan's will doing battle with itself. First, he disobeys the runes on his spear, then he orders Brunhilde (another part of his own self) to set everything right by another betrayal, then he punishes her for interpreting his true wishes aright; then he breeds the race of heroes to succeed and supplant him. Finally, faced by the hero who has at last broken loose from his creator, Wotan becomes Prospero too, then breaks his staff and awaits the end that was always in his beginning."

So, interpreting this potent mythical material as the projection in art form of the fundamental motivating forces of German society in the second half of the nineteenth century and subsequently, we can begin to see something of the daemonic forces threatening eruption in the Kaiserreich and the Weimar Republic and spilling over into Nazism.

We may now turn to a consideration of the personality of Adolf Hitler as a vital part of the psycho-historical interpretation of Germany's recent past. It is to Erik H. Erikson's *Childhood and Society*[33] that we can look for guidance. In Chapter 9, 'The Legend of Hitler's Childhood', there is established that complex connection which links ego-qualities, social institutions and historical eras. "For nations, as well as individuals, are not only defined by their highest point of civilised achievement, but also by the weakest one in their collective identity: they are in fact defined by the distance, and the quality of the distance, between those points." (p.317). This was a truth clearly grasped by Ernst Toller in his ruminative question: "The German in Goethe, in Hölderlin, in Buchner, in Marx — what has that German in common with the 'Dare-men'?"[34] The German nation, personified in its great and ghastly figures (Goethe-Hitler), is best understood and its political life explained as the expression of the conflict between such 'highest points' and 'weakest ones'. When the tension between the two becomes insupportable, as it did in the closing stages of the Weimar Republic, there is a ready welcome for anyone who offers to shoulder the responsibility of bearing that no longer bearable tension. Again, Toller pointed out, "The desire for a dictator is the desire for castration."

In *Mein Kampf* Hitler succeeded at once in setting his story in a mythological key. His readers are invited to tune in to the magic of once-upon-a-time: "In this little town on the river Inn, Bavarian by blood and Austrian by nationality, gilded by the light of German martyrdom there lived at the end of the eighties of last century my parents, the father a faithful servant, the mother devoting herself to the cares of the household and looking after her children with eternally the same loving care." (p.318). What an idyllic picture, somewhat removed from the less seemly realities of Adolf's origins, but calculated to appeal to the longing for the *'gemütlich'*, romanticised fantasies of the German lower bourgeoisie in search of a saviour.

Thomas Mann in a strange little essay entitled, 'Brother Hitler', in which he admitted a shuddering admiration for him, recognised the relationship existing between even the black sheep of the family and his brothers and sisters, though most of them of course identified him as their saviour.

"On the stage of German history Hitler sensed to what extent it was safe to let his own personality represent with hysterical abandon what was alive in every German listener and reader." (p.321) The personal father, whom Adolf represented as 'a faithful civil servant', died when he was still a boy, and this son was certainly not going to be content with being a mere petty official: he wanted to be an artist in spite of paternal disapproval. The collective German father-figure was one of domineering outward authority, so much so that when he came home from work in the evening even the little ornaments on the mantlepiece stood to attention! This characteristic may however be conceived of as concealing a lack of inner authority, which in turn therefore demanded an object or objects on which the inner uncertainty could be projected and transformed by its treatment of them as utterly subservient − a huge exercise in compensation for a serious inferiority complex. The German father's lack of a true inner authority was a lack of "that authority which results from an integration of cultural ideal and educational method". (p.323) This in turn may be thought of as occurring because in collective terms that kind of integration had only occurred in the limited areas of regions and not at all in the Weimar Republic as a generality.

So, Erikson goes on to argue, there developed "a split between precocious individualistic rebellion and disillusioned, obedient citizenship — as a strong factor in the political immaturity of the German." This tendency was of course enormously intensified by the inflation of the 1920s which had virtually wiped out the only source from which such an integration might have come, namely the professional middle classes.

On the feminine side the psychological mechanism at work, both individually in the case of Hitler and collectively in the German people, was for the mother-image to be split into either the Hausfrau, non-political, domesticated cow, or the 'iron virgin', the Valkyrie figure of Brunhilde: Adolf's mother as sketched in *Mein Kampf* and his mistress as personified in Eva Braun on one hand or the tough breeding young mother of the German *Volk* on the other; in the gulf between the two there was no room for an actual, independent self-conscious woman, except occasionally in the Resistance movement.

What begins to emerge with clinical precision is a diagnosis of arrested growth in relationship to parents, the opposite sex and to authority figures in society as a whole. "In Germany then, we saw a highly organised and highly educated nation surrender to the imagery of ideological adolescence . . . historical and geographical realities do amplify familial patterns." (p.335)

Otto Strasser, who first followed and then turned against Hitler, summed up the Führer's shamanistic gifts, embodied chiefly in the growling thunder of his oratory, in the following words: "He touches each private wound in the raw, liberating the mass unconscious, expressing its innermost aspirations, telling it what it most wants to know."

In the early 1930s the German people wanted most to know security, to escape from the murderous legacy of public assassination and street brawling, connected with the deaths of such men as Erzberger and Rathenau and the infamous dealings of the Feme, tribunals of private vengeance and justice swirling up from the Freikorps and the extreme wings of Right and Left.

After fingering the Wagnerian clue and reflecting on the personality of the German dictator, we should now consider the findings of analytical psychology. In his *Farewell to European History*[34] Alfred Weber wrote: "The wing-beat of the dark, daemonic forces: there is no other term for their supra-personal and at once transcendental power." He was referring to those destructive elements in the whole twentieth-century Western civilisation, which found their most appalling and strident expression in the Hitler phenomenon. This has come under searching scrutiny from C. G. Jung in *Civilisation in Transition*.[35] In his essay 'Wotan' (1936 and 1946) Jung puts his finger on the spring of the Nazi movement: "The Hitler movement literally brought the whole of Germany to its feet, from five-year olds to veterans, and produced the spectacle of a nation migrating from one place to another."

Reminding us how traditional forces in Western civilisation, specifically the religious one, had failed to attract and so control the public libido, Jung writes:

"When the Holy Father at Rome could only impotently lament before God the fate of the Grex Segregatus, the one-eyed old hunter, on the edge of the German forest, laughed and saddled Sleipner. . . . Wotan's re-awakening is a stepping back into the past; the stream was dammed up and has broken into its old channel. . . . Wotan is a quite suitable causal hypothesis for explaining the onset of Hitlerian totalitarianism."

"In fact," continues Jung, "I venture the heretical suggestion that the unfathomable depths of Wotan's character explains more of National Socialism than all three reasonable factors put together," that is, the purely political, economic and social. The condition of the mass of the German people under Hitler was one of *Ergriffenheit,* of having been seized, of having been possessed by someone or something: that someone was the Führer, personifying the dark, unconscious side of his own and his people's psyche.

"As an autonomous psychic factor, Wotan produces effects in the collective life of a people and thereby reveals his own nature. . . . Nink in *'Wodam and germanischer Schicksalsglaube'* sketches a really magnificent portrait of the German archetype, Wotan — berserker, god of storms, wanderer, warrior, Wunsch and Minne God, lord of the dead, Einherier, dead hero of Valhalla, magician."

Perhaps the single most clinching piece of evidence regarding the re-animation of twentieth-century German society by the Wotan archetype is provided by the sight of an Evangelical clergyman, Dr Langermann, conducting the funeral service of one, Gustloff, dressed in SS uniform and jackboots, speeding the deceased on his journey to Hades and directing him to Valhalla, to the home of Siegfried and Baldur. "May this God send the nations of this earth clanking on their way through history. Lord bless our struggle." There seems to be little if any lapse between such an invocation and the cries of primitive Teutonic tribes some 1500 years before.

In *After the Catastrophe* Jung was at pains to labour the point that Germany had no monopoly of this 'original sin' or libidinous regression: that was part of the necessary feeling of collective guilt of the West as a whole. "One should not imagine for a moment that anybody could escape this play of opposites. Even a saint would have to pray unceasingly for the souls of Hitler and Himmler, the Gestapo and the SS in order to repair without delay the damage done to his own soul."

The final analysis which Jung offers of the man and the phenomenon is one of hysteria:

"The hysterical disposition consists in the fact that the opposites, inherent in every psyche, and especially those affecting character, are rather more widely apart than in the so-called normal person. This wider separation causes a greater energic tension, which accounts for the German's undeniable energy and proficiency. On the other hand, the greater distance between the opposites occasions greater contradictions in the inner man, conflicts in the field of conscience, disharmonies where the character is concerned, in short all that Goethe's *Faust* represents. Nobody on earth but a German could ever have created such a figure, it is so intrinsically, so infinitely German. In *Faust* we see man 'yearning for the infinite', a longing that flows out of the inner opposition and the tearing asunder, that 'Eros of the distant vision' the eschatological expectation of the great fulfilment. In him we experience the loftiest flights of the mind and the descent into the depths of guilt and darkness, and still worse, a fall so low that it brings man down to the level of wholesale swindle and murderous deeds of violence — the result of the pact with the devil. Faust is also split, and he sets up evil outside himself in the shape of Mephistopheles, to serve as an alibi in case of need . . . he is now driven to admit 'Mephistopheles is my other side, my alter ego, my all too real shadow, that can no longer be denied.' This is not only the fate of Germany, it is also the fate of Europe. We must all open our eyes to the shadow that looms behind the man of today.

"A more accurate diagnosis of Hitler's condition would be pseudologia phantastica, that form of hysteria which is characterised by a peculiar talent for believing one's own lies.

"For this threatened hysteric and transparent impostor was not strutting about on a small stage, but was riding the armoured divisions of the Wehrmacht, with all the weight of German heavy industry behind him."

In a BBC broadcast of 3 November 1946 Jung remarked: "As early as 1918 I noticed a peculiar disturbance in the unconscious of my German patients, which could not be ascribed to their personal psychology." He was referring to that archetypal activity of the unconscious of which Nietzsche fifty or sixty years earlier had had premonition and which he knew would overwhelm the majority of the Germans: he described them in a telling phrase as the *'Zu-kurz-Gekommene'*, those prevented through historical forces at work in the German people from fulfilling their own personal or national destinies.

Before closing this appraisal of the Hitler phenomenon let us first glance back at its origins in the Weimar Republic and then listen in to three more voices, in whose accents we can detect, if we listen attentively enough, the very essence of the psycho-historical truth we are seeking. The period 1919-33 was when the German people, having failed, in Tonnies' concepts, to achieve a true national, democratic *Gemeinschaft* and being unable to function merely as a *Gesellschaft*, had to have recourse to the perversion of a totalitarian *Gemeinschaft*. This was the consequence of heavy casualties in the First World War, their surviving aftermath in the

Freikorps, the quarrelling working class, the disinherited bourgeoisie and finally the wretched unemployed. Listen to Bertholt Brecht in his 'Lied vom SA-Mann', which suggests the mood in which so many people joined the SS.

> *Als mir die Magen knurrte, schlief ich*
> *Vor Hunger ein.*
> *Da hort ich sie ins Ohr mir*
> *Deutschland erwache! schrein.*
> *Da sah ich viele marschieren*
> *Sie sagten: ins Dritte Reich.*
> *Ich hatte nichts zu verlieren*
> *Und lief mit, wohin was mir gleich.*

> From hunger I grew drowsy
> Dulled by my belly's ache
> Then someone shouted in my ear:
> Germany, awake!
> Then I saw many marching
> Towards the Third Reich, they said
> Since I had nought to lose
> I followed where they led.[36]

It is perhaps a legitimate reflection that just as the permissive society of the Weimar Republic refused to or was incapable of dealing with its shadow side and so spawned Nazism, our own contemporary permissive society may be following a similar track.

Listen next to Thomas Mann's character, Zeitblom, in the closing pages of *Dr Faustus;*[37] the artistic vision here illuminates the historical analysis, and we seem to smell the very whiff of the German collapse.

"Since the end of March — it is now the 25th of April this year of destiny 1945 — our resistance in the west has been visibly disintegrating. The papers, already half-unmuzzled, register the truth. Rumour, fed by enemy announcements on the radio and stories told by fugitives, knows no censorship, but carries the individual details of swiftly spreading catastrophe about the land, into regions not yet swallowed, not yet liberated by it, and even hither into my retreat. No hold any more: everybody surrenders, everybody runs away. Our shattered, battered cities fall like ripe plums. Darmstadt, Wurzburg, Frankfurt are gone; Mannheim and Cassel, even Munster and Leipzig are in foreign hands. One day the English reached Bremen, the Americans were at the gates of Upper Franconia; Nuremberg, city of the national celebrations so uplifting to unenlightened hearts, Nuremberg surrendered. The great ones of the régime, who wallowed in power, riches and wrong, now rage and kill themselves: justice is done. Russian corps, after taking Königsberg and Vienna were free to force the Oder; they moved a million strong against the capital, lying in its rubble, already abandoned by all the government officials. Russian troops carried out with their heavy artillery the sentence long since inflicted from the air. They are now approaching the centre of Berlin. Last year the horrible man escaped with his life — by now surely an insanely flaring and flickering existence — from the plot of desperate patriots trying to salvage the future of Germany and the last remnant of her material goods. Now he has commanded his soldiery to drown in a sea of blood the attack on Berlin and to shoot every officer who speaks of surrender. And the order has been in considerable measure obeyed. At the same time strange radio messages in German, no longer quite sane, rove the upper air; some of them commend the population to the benevolence of the conquerors, even including the secret police, who they say have been much slandered. Others are transmitted by a 'Freedom Movement' christened Werwolf: a band of raving mad lads who hide in the woods and break out nightly; they have already deserved well of the Fatherland by many a gallant murder of the invaders. The fantastic mingles with the horrible: up to the very end the crudely legendary, the grim deposit of saga in the soul of the nation, is involved, with all its familiar echoes and reverberations.

"A transatlantic general has forced the population of Weimar to file past the crematories of the neighbouring concentration camps. He declared that these citizens, who had gone in apparent righteousness about their daily concerns and sought to know nothing, although the wind brought to their noses the stench of burning human flesh — he declared that they too were guilty of the abominations on which he forced them to now turn their eyes. Was that unjust? Let them look, I look with them. In spirit I let myself be shouldered in their dazed or shuddering ranks. Germany had become a thick-walled underground torture-chamber, converted into one by the profligate dictatorship vowed to nihilism from its beginnings on. Now the torture-chamber has been broken open, open lies our shame before the eyes of the world. Foreign commissions inspect those incredible photographs everywhere displayed, and tell their countrymen that what they have seen surpasses in horribleness anything the human imagination can conceive. I say our shame. For is it mere hypochondria to say to oneself that everything German, even the German mind and spirit, German thought, the German word, is involved in this scandalous exposure and made subject to the same distrust? Is the sense of guilt quite morbid which makes one ask oneself the question how Germany, whatever her future manifestations, can ever presume to open her mouth in human affairs?

"Let us call them the sinister possibilities of human nature in general that here come to light. German human beings, tens of thousands, hundreds of thousands of them it is, who have perpetrated what humanity shudders at; and all that is German now stands forth as an abomination and a warning. How will it be to belong to a land whose history witnesses this hideous default: a land self-maddened, psychologically burnt out, which quite understandably despairs of governing itself and thinks it for the best that it became a colony of foreign powers; a nation that will have to live shut in like the ghetto of the Jews, because a frightfully swollen hatred round all its borders will not permit it to emerge; a nation that cannot show its face outside?

"Curses, curses on the corrupters of an originally decent species of human being, law-abiding, only too docile, only all too willingly living on theory, who thus went to school to Evil! How good it is to curse — or rather how good it would be, if only the cursing came from a free and unobstructed heart! We are present at the last gasp of a blood state which, as Luther put it, 'took on its shoulders' immeasurable crimes; which roared and bellowed to the ravished and reeling masses proclamation cancelling all human rights; which set up its gaudy banners for youth to march under, and they marched, with proud tread and flashing eyes, in pure and ardent faith.

But a patriotism which would assert that a blood state like that was so forced, so foreign to our national character that it could not take root among us: such a patriotism would seem to me more high-minded than realistic. For was this government, in word and deed, anything but the distorted, vulgarised, besmirched symbol of a state of mind, a notion of world affairs which we must recognise as both genuine and characteristic? Indeed, must not the Christian and humane man shrink as he sees it stamped upon the features of our greatest, the mightiest embodiments of our essential Germanness? I ask — and should I not? Ah, it is no longer in question that this beaten people now standing wild-eyed in face of the void stand there just because they have failed, failed horribly in their last and uttermost attempt to find the political form suited to their particular needs."

Listen finally, this time once again to Albert Speer, an actual historical person, not a character of fiction. His Faust-like pact with Hitler in aid of the forwarding of his own architectural ambitions was to lead him to become Nazi Minister of Production and Armaments, an accomplice to atrocity, condemned at the Nuremberg trial for war criminals, to twenty years' imprisonment and at last a commendably honest autobiography of contrition and perspicacity. Speer points once again to the defects of Weimar:

"Our German teacher, an enthusiastic democrat, often read aloud to us from the liberal *Frankfurter Zeitung*. But for this teacher I would have remained altogether non-political in school. For we were being educated in terms of a conservative bourgeois view of the world. In spite of the Revolution which had brought in the Weimar Republic, it was still impressed upon us that the distribution of power in society and the traditional authorities were part of the God-given order of things!" (p.7)

Speer notes the fatal flaw in the 'non-political' German citizen: "Years later in Spandau I read Ernst Cassirer's comment on the men who of their own accord threw away man's highest privilege: to be an autonomous person." (p.49)

Speer speaks with moving sincerity of himself, and for most of his fellow-Germans of the period 1918-45: "But when I think over my life up to and including the years of imprisonment, there was no period in which I was free from delusory notions." (p.291) Such delusory notions had their springs, as we have seen, in the German unconscious, and precipitated the Hitler phenomenon.

The German Resistance and Adolf Reichwein: The General Picture

It has been established that without doubt there was a German Resistance movement against the Hitler régime. It proceeded from those who were not too 'psychologically dissociated' that is, well enough integrated as persons, to recognise what was happening and who had sufficient courage to do something about it. Adolf Reichwein was such a person, whose individual fate we shall be following in detail. For some resisters it was necessary that they should receive supportive encouragement from a political or religious institution, while others acted more from private initiative.

The German Resistance was made up, as in the Resistance movements of other countries, of various strands, but in two respects it was utterly unlike them. First, it received no help from the Allied powers, and secondly it failed. It had to operate moreover within the interstices of a totalitarian state, and its pathos, dignity, frequent inefficiency and eventual lack of success did and does raise the question of just how it is possible to organise resistance against a totalitarian state once it is firmly established. Prior to the outbreak of war in 1939 it must be admitted that the German people consisted of a large number, the majority, who were satisfied with if not enthusiastic about the Hitler régime, and an uneasy minority who chose one of two alternatives, either *'aussere Emigration'*, that is emigration overseas, or *'innere imigration'*, that is, withdrawal from public life in an attempt simply to cultivate their own gardens, and lastly a tiny minority who both before and during the war worked actively against the régime and plotted to overthrow it. Reichwein became one of these.

What were the human constituents of that tiny minority? Harold Poelchau, prison chaplain and pastor to some eighty anti-Hitler conspirators, said in a radio address on 20 July 1946:

"They consisted of a wide variety of men, coming from all quarters: from industry and administration like Goerdeler, from agriculture like the big peasant, Wenzel Teutschental, from the Christian trade unions like Niklas Gross, the miner and editor, from the Socialist trade unions, like Theodor Haubach, Julius Leber and Hermann Maass, from the army like Generals Olbricht, Beck and many others, from the churches like Father Delp and the still surviving Father Rosch and Dr Gerstenmaier, from diplomacy like Adam von Trott and Hans von Haeften, from education like Adolf Reichwein, liberal middle-class men like Minister Popitz and Socialist conservatives like Counts Yorck and Molte."[38]

Enlightening studies of the frightful predicament in which decent, intelligent Germans were placed are to be found in Christopher Sykes' *Troubled Loyalty: A Biography of Adam von Trott*,[39] and *The Past is Myself*[40] by Christabel Bielenberg, an English woman married to a German involved in the Resistance.

The problems of unity among this varied band, not least in their swaying attitude toward communism and the Soviet Union, were highlighted by the dubious relationship in which they stood to Die Rote Kapelle, a German communist organisation which often acted as a spy agency for the USSR. Undoubtedly the most moving expression of young people's attempts at Resistance was the Munich students' protest under Sophie and Hans Scholl, Die Weisse Rose. Some idea of the scale of the Resistance movement can be obtained from the following figures which belong to the Gestapo files of August 1942:

Germans arrested for downing tools	1,761
Germans arrested for illegal contacts with foreign workers	1,583
Germans detained as Marxists	1,210
Germans detained as Reactionaries	1,267
Germans detained as Resisters	1,007
Total	6,828

These were those of course who were caught. The total number must be assumed to have been very much greater.

The culmination of the efforts of those who actively tried to prevail against Hitler was the plot on his life (incidentally one of many) of 20 July 1944. It had both military and civil components: to the former belonged Beck, Von Tresckow and supremely, Graf Klaus Schenck von Stauffenberg, who actually carried the bomb into the Führer's headquarters on the Eastern Front; to the latter belong the Social Democrat Julius Leber, the conservative Goerdeler, the diplomat Ulrich von Hassell. Operation Valkyrie, as it was somewhat incongruously referred to, was a disastrous and tragic failure. Hitler, though badly shaken, survived with minor injuries, the army wavered in its allegiances, the Nazi government kept control of the situation and apprehended very many of the conspirators. One of the noblest of these was Helmut James Graf von Moltke (1907-44) whose *Last Letters* make poignant reading and may be taken as a symbol of the heroic, often inefficient and certainly ineffective attempts of the better elements in Germany to struggle against the nightmare of totalitarian oppression. As he himself remarked on one occasion: "The measure of our immortality is the frequency of our immortal actions."

Adolf Reichwein

Born in 1898, Reichwein was in his youth a keen Wandervögel, who fought briefly in the First World War, was wounded and in 1918-19 took up his studies in Marburg and Frankfurt. From 1923 to 1926 he worked as an organiser of adult education in Thuringia and travelled adventurously in the USA and the Far East. He also became Press Secretary to Carl Heinrich Becker, the Minister of Education in Prussia, and from 1927 until 1933 he held the Chair of Political Science at the University of Halle. With Hitler's coming to power, Reichwein refused the opportunity to emigrate, even though his outspoken anti-Nazi views were well-known. Instead, on dismissal from his professorship, he persuaded the somewhat astonished Nazi authorities to let him take up an appointment as headmaster of a primary school in Tiefensee about forty miles east of Berlin. Here he lived from 1933 to 1939 with his second wife and growing family, experimenting in educational methods and maintaining contact with a wide circle of politically like-minded friends all over Germany. In

1939 he succeeded in getting himself put in charge of the school section of the Deutsches Museum in Berlin where he continued until his death. He used this office as a cover for his Resistance work — the curator became conspirator.

A friend, referring to Reichwein's work both as village schoolmaster and museum curator, wrote:

"It was the cloak, daily becoming thinner, for his own passionate activity. His professional demotion had not injured him as a person; he had disciplined himself to take hard knocks. In addition he at first retained the admiration of his opponents and so managed to gain from them a sphere of activity and their grudging respect. But the Socialist in him was deeply outraged by the pseudo-Socialism of Hitler, the German by the distortion and disfigurement of German art, the lover of truth by the deceitful and perverted misuse of true values, the free man by suppression of free speech, the humanitarian by brute power. At first he hoped that the thunder clouds would soon pass, that in the meantime he could take shelter in the kind of work he was doing and then start again when the air was cleared; for a long time he underestimated the cold consequences of pure will-to-power and the daemonism of imprisoned forces, which were at work in it. But the more Germany was dazzled by it, the more disorder broke loose and the more threatening the evil became, so the more determined grew his resistance every day. He began by making thorough enquiries as to the whereabouts, outlook and occupation and 'cover' of old acquaintances. Of these only a few had to be let go, while new ones were added to them, so that the net of his contacts became finer rather than coarser."

At the beginning of the year 1941 Reichwein was refreshing himself with a skiing holiday in order that up in the mountains, as he put it, 'I may become a more normal man again.' He wrote to a friend:

"With each person we lose, the burden on our own shoulders becomes heavier — it can only become lighter if we actually realise this and feel committed. In the last resort, all of us, the dead as well as the living, serve the same eternal cause, namely to roll aside from mankind the fantastically heavy tombstone which presses on it, so that men really can be men. Let us draw closer to one another — in death as well as in life."

Elsewhere he remarked:

"It is really the most profound subjects for the sake of which we act at the surface level, and we must always remain conscious of this relationship between the two. Then there are no superficialities left, and everything we do is important in so far as it is related to fundamentals. Surely the Germans taken as a whole are the most fundamental of all Western peoples. If only this creative thoroughness could be brought into vital relationship with political endeavour."

In the last sentence Reichwein was touching one of the nucleii of the 'German problem', and during this year and subsequently he was actively trying to solve it for himself and others by the increasing part he played in political consultation and planning.

At this point it is necessary to consider the particular role played by the Kreisau Circle in the German Resistance Movement. It came into existence and started systematic discussions in the summer of 1940. It consisted of conservatives and socialists, propertied gentry and Trade Unionists, Protestants and Catholics. They were united by a common desire to see the end of the Nazis, but some, probably the majority at least until quite near to 20 July 1944, were primarily concerned with plans for the creation of democratic government and postwar reconstruction in Germany after the anticipated Allied defeat of Hitler. The attitude towards the army generals of these elements and of the minority within the group who favoured active conspiracy to assassinate the tyrant and their potential as colleagues always remained ill-defined.

The three premises from which the group set out were as follows: National Socialism was an absolute departure from German and European traditions and a denial of the Christian and humanist conception of man; Germany's military position was hopeless but that the onset of military defeat constituted great dangers to Germany and to central Europe which it was the duty of every responsible person to guard

against; and lastly, since any large, organised, political opposition in Germany was in the circumstances of 1940 out of
the question, it was recognised that new forms of activity
must be discovered. The agreed policy decisions were listed
under the headings of reconstruction of the state, industry,
church and educational institutions, the judicial treatment of
war criminals and offenders against the laws of the state. The
group felt that attempts made by oecumenical circles to
establish contact with the Allies had done more harm than
good, and that it was unrealistic of the Allies to expect any
active military movement against the régime in Germany.
Obviously within the Kreisau Circle there were conflicts of
opinion, for example as to whether violence was justified in
the removal of a tyrant and also as to whether Germany's
interests would best be served by seeking contacts with
Russia and the East or with the Western powers. It never
really made up its mind whether it was a conspiracy or a
preparatory commission discussing postwar reconstruction; it
seemed to be concerned with what some of its members
called 'a directed defeat'. Wheeler-Bennett in *The Nemesis of
Power*[41] wrote somewhat harshly of the Kreisau Circle as
"the conscientious objectors of the Resistance" and of
Moltke and Yorck that "Their remedy, however, was little
more than an amalgam of Prussian mysticism and Prussian
Christian Socialism". Yet from a study of their endeavours
there emerges quite unmistakably a sense of heroism and
self-sacrifice and a quality of nobility, which gives to the
whole Kreisau enterprise a touch of tragic splendour. As
Marion Grafin Yorck remarked in her widowhood, "When
their lives were demanded of them, they surrendered them
without knowing whether their deaths would bear any visible
fruit, but each one of them offered his life as penance for a
commonly shared and acknowledged guilt."

It is into a climate of opinion such as that hinted at above
that we must think of Reichwein entering with his established reputation as a pedagogue. From his correspondence
we catch glimpses of him during the spring and early summer
months of 1942, busy with his triple task of looking after his
family in their and his increasingly enforced and frequent
absences from Berlin, broadening his contacts with indivi-

duals pledged to resist the Nazis and carrying out his official duties. In a letter of April 1943 Reichwein writes: "One notices that we have no friends in the world, whose hearts might be moved by our fate." In August and September he went on tour lecturing to the Forces first in the USSR and then in Paris: "Parisians still know how to live in spite of misery and shortages: at weekends they travel into Normandy to fetch butter and eggs, and they have not surrendered their basic optimism. But as a German in this half-dead city, one has one's own secret thoughts."

Meanwhile his wife and children, bombed out from their Berlin home, had taken refuge on the Kreisau estate in East Prussia. In April and May 1944 Reichwein was travelling in South Germany, spending Whitsuntide with his family at Kreisau. These months were charged with intense, political activity and culminated in his arrest by the Gestapo at the beginning of July. From then until his brutal execution on 20 October 1944, he was in the hands of the Nazis, imprisoned and tortured. His letters of farewell to wife and children were grave, tender and encouraging, as two extracts illustrate:

"I need hardly say that my thoughts are constantly taken up with my own past life. But I can't really write about that now, however beneficial it might be. One thing stands out clearly from contemplating those past decades — how rich and beautiful the time has been for me! The pain of the First World War fades into insignificance and the healthy country life of an unfettered youth shines out all the more brightly — the ten years with the Wandervögel and the excursions, near and far — the friendships of youth-happy student days in Frankfurt and Marburg with yet other indissoluble friendships — then my enthusiastically lived professional existence in adult education, the exceptional privileges of my travels in Europe, Asia and America, four years of flying and looking down on the earth from an eagle's perspective — in between academic work, which cost nights as well as days of labour, and finally the loveliest and richest of all — twelve years with you and the children. How much cause I have to be thankful!"

And then an the eve of his execution:

"My dear Romai,

Judgement has been passed. For the last time I am writing your name, which has become so precious to me. In this last hour of mine on earth my thoughts are turning ever again with special intimacy to you and the four children, who you gave me and who for years, which to me seem many, were such a joy, comfort and edification. These three months have been a time of great inner significance to me in spite of all the pain: they have helped to clarify and, I hope, also to purify a great deal. I depart with calm because I know that the children are in your care. Since 5 July my daily prayer has been the Our Father and, attached to it a petition for you, the children and our parents. It is to this prayer that I owe my strength from day to day.

May God give you the strength to overcome difficulties and to continue your life steadfastly. Let the children, as they grow into the future, be your consolation and then your joy. Thank your parents, relations and friends for all their goodness. For you my whole heart,

Your own Adolf"

A Latvian exile who only encountered Reichwein in Berlin in 1943 and 1944 has left us this testimony:

"It is rare to come across men in whom idealism and patriotism shine forth so clearly, whose devotion to their countrymen and their belief in equal rights for all enable them to meet the greatest dangers intrepidly. His warm sympathy for my own fate soon led to a close friendship between us. Professor Reichwein was a convinced German patriot. He believed that God had set the German people as any other to fulfil a mission, which it must complete, not however by repressing other peoples but by cooperating with them. I met Professor Reichwein for the last time at the end of June 1944, when he said, 'Decisive steps must be taken to rescue the German people and European culture. It is tragic that we have to have recourse to means, which the whole of my inner conviction rejects. At best we shall no longer have any private life — that we must sacrifice for the sake of our children and the future of the German people. For the very sake of that future, so it must be. Already it is late, very late, but still not too late. Very soon now you'll see another

Germany, and this new Germany will have quite a different attitude towards your country than the present one has.' It was only after the attempted coup of 20 July 1944 became known that I fully understood those words. And when, later I received a short message saying, 'Professor Reichwein is no longer alive', I knew that there was one less noble spirit in the world."

The life and death of Adolf Reichwein provide suggestive commentary on a fundamental problem of this age, namely the totalitarian sickness of society. Within a German setting they illustrate three aspects of a more than German pheno-menon: first, the very nature of totalitarianism itself, secondly the impossibility of its being resisted when once established by traditional methods of statecraft, and thirdly the need for a creative response to its challenge, which by accepting the daemonic elements inherent in it, is enabled to transcend them and so to pass beyond resistance. Faustian man has need of Mephistopheles in his quest for self-knowledge: the 'shadow' which his being casts takes on the form of an objective reality, apparently external to himself, in the case of the Nazi, the Jew. The integration of his personality occurs where that is assimilated which was pre-viously projected, thus in the language of Blake, 'destroying the negative to redeem the contraries'. It may well be that Europe and many other parts of the world stand in need of the German examples as the means whereby they can learn how to redeem their own bodies politic by accepting the daemonic forces within them. Reichwein and other men of good will of his generation had some insight into the problems to which totalitarianism proposed a specious answer: they tried for a time to disentangle the true from the false in that process. Because they lacked the psychological wisdom to transcend the brute contradictions with which totalitarianism surely confronted them, they were eventually bound to shape their resistance in a manner which could only end in disaster. That was their tragedy; by a just appraisal of their fate it can become our opportunity, for, as Abbot remarked, "The use of History is to light the present hour to its duty."

The impossibility of the German Resistance movement

showed itself nowhere more clearly than in its diffuse nature: it could be described as consisting of resistance by intention and resistance by deed, if we leave aside the absurdity of those many thousands of Germans who after the event claimed to have been resisters all the time! Reichwein started by belonging to the former category and passed into the second. He realised that in the German society of his time there was a need of men and women who had the capacity "To break with yesterday without already possessing tomorrow", a demand however which means mature citizens; otherwise those who have been dislodged from yesterday without their consent merely revert to many days before yesterday when faced with the unacceptable challenge of tomorrow — the fate of most Hitler-worshippers. The degree of 'compromise' with the Nazism which Reichwein had to make during his period at Tiefensee and Berlin is yet another illustration of the impossibility of uncompromising resistance to totalitarianism: either the compromise does not last, as in Reichwein's case, or else it becomes acquiescent collusion. Education might be the long-term answer to the causes of totalitarianism, but the latter was itself destructive of any such long-term project. So Reichwein took up his double life of curator and conspirator and found himself, however reluctantly, like others in the Kreisau Circle, compelled to transmute his impatience and agony over the last days of the Nazi régime into that active conspiracy which was to cost him his life. This was because he must have realised the basic lack of realism in all the making of blueprints for Germany after Hitler's defeat, when that defeat was not really desired by the bulk of the nation for the right reasons.

Reichwein then was a minority figure involved in the impossibility of resistance to Nazism, politically a failure, educationally of some consequence, personally of fine, human quality, whose most obvious legacy was to be seen in the small but not uninfluential group of educators in postwar Germany who remember him with respect and affection. "In May of the year 1946," wrote a youth-time friend of Reichwein's, "I encountered a working-man at a level-crossing in the neighbourhood of Friedberg/Hessen, who addressed me in a friendly fashion and turned out to be a former comrade of the First World War. In the course of conversation he asked after Adolf Reichwein: he had a lively recollection of him. Yet more than twenty-five years had gone by since the time from which this memory arose. What an impression Reichwein must have made on that nineteen-year-old contemporary of his and how often must Reichwein's image have bubbled up in the thoughts of this simple man! Not only that — he had got a firm grasp of the personality of that more mature comrade, by whom he had been consciously influenced in several decisive moments of his life, and there must have been very many more unconsciously so influenced! When I told him about Reichwein's death, his simple comment was: 'For me he remains what he was.' But who was he? This is a question that cannot be disposed of by listing his intellectual, pedagogical and academic achievements: it leads us on to the totality of a personality. Without knowing anything of Reichwein's cultural gifts, that labourer had been permanently affected by his 'mere existence'. The life of a man like Reichwein sends its ripples of creative reality into the lives of his fellow-men and so out into the whole world. A truly lived existence has no end, just as it has no clearcut beginning. Its spiritual essence is variable but not transient. Such a life strengthens one's belief in the elemental existence of spirit and triumph over death, just as supernatural religion maintains it does."

Psycho-history studies these ripples in the conviction that it is their contents which constitute historical reality.

Germany since 1945: the Events of Twenty-seven Years

When Germany surrendered to the Allies in May 1945, many of her cities were in ruins, her war-production plants had practically come to a halt, and the Nazi régime was discredited. It should, however, be remembered that unlike some of her enemies, Britain, France and the Soviet Union in particular, it was only in the closing months of the struggle that the majority of the German population had begun to suffer from material shortages. The position of the four main victorious powers was paradoxical: on the one hand their shared objective was to prevent the resurgence of Germany as a dominating force in Europe and to instil into her a democratic form of government, on the other there was basic disagreement on ideological grounds between the three Western democracies and the USSR about future frontiers, for example, the Oder-Neisse line, the nature of democracy and the relationship of the USSR and the USA to one another as world powers. The Cold War, anticipated at Yalta, began at Potsdam.

The years from 1945 to 1949 may properly be thought of as the period of Allied occupation. Territorially the main feature of this was the dissolution of Prussia, with the Poles moving into Silesia and Eastern Pomerania to the Oder-Neisse line, the handing over of the Saar to France, which lasted until 1957, and the division of the whole of the rest of Germany into four zones of occupation, Russian, American, British and French, with the city of Berlin as an enclave of its own within the Russian zone but administered jointly by a four-power commission. The opening months of this phase were marked by efforts of all four Allied powers at denazi-fication, an extremely complex and often frustrating enter-prise due to the difficulty of deciding exactly what had constituted being a Nazi and the need to man in skeleton form the German administrative system at land and local levels. As this was accompanied by attempts by each of the four occupying powers to introduce their own particular version of democracy, and as in the Soviet Zone this naturally took the form of a totalitarian democracy, develop-ments occurred which often took strange and contradictory forms. One is tempted to recall Lord Haldane's remark and contrast it with the position pertaining in Germany then, namely that parliamentary democracy is only possible when the Government meets the Opposition out at dinner!

Meanwhile at Nuremberg the leading Nazi figures were placed on trial for crimes against humanity. Some were executed, Goering committed suicide, Krupp was imprisoned, as were Hess and Speer. Von Papen, Schacht and General Fritzsch were found not guilty!

Gradually the Allies permitted the recreation of German political parties, of which the most important in the West were the Christian Democratic Union and the Social Demo-cratic Party and in the East the Socialist Unity Party. In 1947 President Truman stated his doctrine of help to all dem-ocratic countries in need, and Marshall Aid for the economic recovery of Europe including Germany was launched. In June

1948 there was a much needed currency reform in the West, which among other things led to such a deterioration of East-West relations among the Allies that the Russians decided to blockade Berlin. From June 1948 to May 1949 the beleaguered city was supplied by a gigantic airlift on the part of the Western powers: Operation Victuals! After this, and with Allied approval in the Western zones, there was increasing independence for the Germans and moves towards the unification of the Länder through the creation of a Parliamentary Council, which was to be the forerunner of a fully sovereign state.

At this stage it is convenient to summarise the developments of Western and Eastern Germany separately. Bonn became the capital of the German Federal Republic, which under the Presidency of Heuss and the patriarchal administration of Konrad Adenauer, successively and successfully dealt with the problem of its refugees from Eastern Germany and the restoration of its economic life, the so-called economic miracle, more rationally explicable in terms of American aid and the fact that German industry having been largely destroyed could be re-equipped with the latest machinery. These events culminated in the Deutschland Vertrag ending the Occupation Statute in the West in May 1952. With her entry into the European Common Market, the compensation paid to her surviving Jews or the relatives of those who had perished, the apparent Allied need of her as a military partner and therefore her rearmament, the Federal Republic had become a recognised, full member of the comity of nations within eight years of her shattering defeat. Here was a curious commentary on the predictions of Zeitblom in Mann's *Dr Faustus*, who, however, was perhaps not so far off the mark when we consider that Germany had in fact been split into two halves.

The great unresolved problem, symbolised by the divided city of Berlin, was the reunification of the two halves of Germany. In 1955 the German Federal Republic joined NATO and the German Democratic Republic joined the Warsaw Pact countries. The long, solid rule of Adenauer (1876-1969), who still had an absolute majority in 1957, was beginning to be challenged by a revived Social Democratic Party under the dynamic leadership of Brandt, the colourful and courageous mayor of West Berlin. In August 1961 the Russians insisted on the Berlin Wall being built as a physical barrier to check the flow of manpower from the German Democratic Republic westwards. Adenauer in his last years achieved a close understanding with de Gaulle, thus apparently ending for ever the age-old Franco-German enmity. After the two chancellorships of Erhard and Kiesinger, 1965-9, Brandt became Chancellor in 1969 and set in train his Ostpolitik, a resolute and realistic attempt to achieve some form of agreement with the German Democratic Republic under Soviet approval regarding the future of Berlin and the gradual removal of obstacles to intercourse between Germans in East and West Germany. This initiative was still very much in the air, as Brandt's right-wing critics tried in the spring of 1972 to thwart it, but without success.

The German Democratic Republic, which was established under Soviet tutelage in October 1949, was and is a monolithic totalitarian communist state. In spite of very hard material conditions and considerable political oppression, which was reflected in the protest uprising of the German workers in January 1953, which was suppressed, the régime gradually established itself under the iron rule of Ulbricht. In 1971 he was succeeded by Honecker as head of the ruling party, but still the whole ethos of the German Democratic Republic differs fundamentally from that of the German Federal Republic, both of them reflecting and participating in the great power ideological struggle of the world scene. Whether Brandt's Ostpolitik succeeds must depend in the last resort on factors which lie partly outside German domestic politics.

The Interpretations of Psycho-History
In attempting interpretation it is useful to build a bridge between the years 1933-45 and the postwar period, constructed out of the ongoing opposition to totalitarian forces in Germany. One, in the shape of Adolf Reichwein's career, has already been sketched, but it is worthwhile to reflect further on the psycho-social condition of the German people at the end of the Hitler nightmare. For German reaction to the July 1944 plot and the German Resistance movement became an ambivalent one, and this ambivalence itself had

two ingredients. From the point of view of the German Democratic Republic the only opposition which was credited with any serious motive and drive was the communist section of it. Within the German Federal Republic there were those who looked on men like Moltke, Stauffenberg and Leber as heroes, but there were also those who regarded the conspirators, particularly the soldiers among them, as traitors to their country. Moreover it cannot be denied that a number of Germans, especially during the period of the Allied occupation, made out that they had really been on the side of the Resistance all the time. Günther Grass in his novel *The Tin Drum*,[42] who himself became an active political supporter of the new democratic forces in the German Federal Republic, had some cutting comments on this theme:

"That word, 'resistance', has become very fashionable. We hear of 'the spirit of resistance', of 'resistance circles'. There is even talk of an 'inward resistance', 'a psychic emigration'. Not to mention those courageous and uncompromising souls who call themselves Resistance Fighters, Men of the Resistance, because they were fined during the war for not blacking out their bedroom windows properly." (p.116)

Nevertheless, as has already been amply demonstrated, there was a genuine Resistance movement inside Germany, but so great were its casualties at Hitler's hands that very few survived to play their part in the post-Hitler period of reconstruction. It is well worth recalling here another actual German emigration activity, which did succeed with British assistance in sustaining itself creatively while in exile in England, in preparing for the restoration of true education in a Germany once defeated and in actually sending back a number of its leading members to hold key positions in their native country. This was a body which called itself German Educational Reconstruction, and its story supplies an unique cultural footnote to the political and economic aspects of our theme. "The sustaining force and inspiration of GER lay in the informed compassion of a few hundred private individuals, who saw that a job needed to be done and who possessed the skill and the determination to translate that vision into actuality." Formed in the early stages of the Second World War by German educationists enjoying political asylum in Britain, together with a few British educational and social workers, GER arranged conferences and set some of its members to work on publications, above all reading sheets, for emergency use by German children as soon as hostilities ceased. Some members lectured to their often disillusioned fellow-countrymen, who had become prisoners of war. As the war drew to a close, contacts were established with government departments and later with the Allied Control Commission. Books, periodicals, writing materials were collected in Britain and shipped to Germany by the ton. German educationists came over to Britain to study educational institutions there. Then in the 1950s the traffic began to flow the other way, and British educationists and returning German teachers entered on the German educational scene with modest but undeniable effect.[43] Yet this bridge, two slender girders of which have been mentioned in the Resistance legacy and in GER, had to span a colossal gulf of non-communication between generations, classes, parties and regions. As a German professor remarked in 1949, "For us Germans Goethe is no alibi: between Goethe and us lies Buchenwald." That remark epitomises what Germans call the problem of the 'unmastered past', *'die unbewältigte Vergangenheit'*: to that problem which still remains with Germany, whether in a political form — the divided country — or in more subtle, deeper ways, we shall now bend our attention. In so doing we shall be picking up once again that Ariadne thread by means of which we are trying to find our way through the labyrinth of German psycho-history: it is the overall human problem cast in a German setting of authoritarianism.

"The moral man commands himself," wrote Herbart, but this accomplishment demands great powers of self-discipline both in the individual and the collective. Where and when for any reason that self-discipline is unavailable or not forthcoming, authority is inevitably projected and takes shape in an external authority figure. So it was with Weimar and the Hitler régime, and we can follow its course by means of a remarkable novel by Siegfried Lenz, curiously and significantly entitled *The German Lesson.*[44] It deals with those feelings of guilt aroused by the inability to master that supreme lesson of self-discipline.

The time of the story is 1954, and Siggi Jepson, its leading character, is detained in a penal settlement for juvenile delinquents. Note that Günther Grass's hero in *The Tin Drum* makes his appraisal of the German question from the ward of a lunatic asylum. It is interesting that both authors felt the need for distancing techniques in order to master the past. Siggi, it is hoped, will be cured of his affliction, which is a mania for stealing pictures. Part of his institutional assignment is to write an essay on 'The Joys of Duty', and this develops into the book itself. Its subject matter is the history of his father, "the northernmost policeman in Germany", stationed in Schleswig Holstein and devoted to his duties. The Nazi authorities order him to see that the celebrated painter, Nansen, does not commit any further paintings. Nansen, we are told, has become "Alienated from the healthy instinct of the people — a danger to the state and undesirable, simply degenerate". Actually he is a mythologising pantheist of the North German landscape, but he blotted his copy book way back in 1934 by declining official honours on the grounds of a disabling allergy to the colour brown!

The policeman, in spite of his long-standing personal friendship with Nansen, carries out his duties meticulously and relentlessly, but the painter continues to paint. The father tries to enlist Siggi's aid: "A useful chap is a chap who toes the line. We'll make a useful chap of you yet, you'll see." But Siggi is on Nansen's side and helps him to preserve his paintings. Even after the end of the war the sinister influence of the policeman's duty-needing personality makes him go on persecuting Nansen, and Siggi starts rescuing the paintings by stealing them from art galleries. Then the author with great skill switches his focus, and we are shown the city-slickers, exemplified in the art critic, Maltzahn, who are trying to exploit the now fashionable anti-Nazi trends of postwar Germany. Maltzahn had edited a magazine called *Art and the People* under the Nazis and had attacked Nansen's paintings as a 'witches' sabbath'. After the war he emerges as editor of a magazine called *Abiding Things,* enthusiastically praising Nansen's work. As D. J. Enright wrote in an appreciative review (*Listener,* 9 March 1972):

"Furthermore, Lenz demonstrates the superior effectiveness

in art of the hint. One day after the end of the war the train draws in and deposits a legless man. 'Albrecht Isenbuttel,' remarkes a bystander. 'So he did get back from Leningrad alive.' His wife, pregnant by her Belgian POW worker, lifts him onto his home-made wooden cart. She looks at his stumps, he looks at her swollen belly, neither says a word. Then there is Klaas, Siggi's elder brother, who deserted from the Army and whom the policeman refuses to take back into the family even though Klaas might now be viewed as a hero of the Resistance: 'The times may have changed, but what you did — there's no changing that.' Klaas, we gather from remarks dropped by Nansen, has had his adventures, but the story of them is left untold. For one thing Siggi would have been too young to grasp what was happening and Lenz prefers to use him in rather the same way that Grass uses children in *Dog Years:* 'Bet you it's bones. And what's more human bones.' The novel isn't softened by the absence of explicit horrors: there is no fairy-tale flavour, nor do the characters decline into allegorical types. Indeed towards the end there comes a bitter taste of realism when a new generation of painters find old Nansen little more than a 'cosmic window-dresser', and one of them, himself, a dedicated artist, considers it his duty to beat up Siggi for obstinately defending 'the greatest of cloud-cuckoo painters'. Sweetness and light are more easily found among the opportunists than the dutiful.''

Thus we are enabled to begin savouring the atmosphere of postwar Germany in the Federal Republic, understanding something of the legacies it inherited from previous events.

As Michael Balfour puts it in his fine study, *West Germany:*[45]

"In Wagner's Ring of the Nibelungs Wotan steals the pure and noble gold from the depths of the Rhine so as to fashion for himself a ring which will confer world mastery. But Alberich lays the curse of death on everyone into whose possession the Ring comes. Only when the Ring is restored to the river from which it was taken, can peace return to the world."

The greatest creative artist to be born in Germany in the nineteenth century based his masterpiece on an allegory only too applicable to the history of his own nation. For it is indeed the German desire for world mastery which has done so much to bring the curse of death upon the world. Twice the lust of Germans for a position which they did not have the necessary strength to achieve and which the rest of mankind would never have allowed them to retain, has shaken the social order of the West to its foundations and endangered the survival of civilised life.

The main question which must therefore come to the mind of anyone studying contemporary Germany is whether the Ring has been returned to the Rhine. Has the German nation abandoned its exaggerated ambitions and is it prepared for the future to be content with a position proportionate to its resources? (p.131)

Because not so many years ago it looked as if a neo-Nazi movement might be in embryonic formation in the shape of the FDP (Freie Demokratische Partei), an extreme right-wing group, it is worth taking a sounding on this point with the help of Jurgen Nevu-du-Mont, a German television commentator. His book *After Hitler: Report from a West German City*[46] is a study of a cross-section of the population of Heidelberg. Stefan Stein, aged thirty-nine (therefore born about 1930 with youth and adolescence in the Third Reich) comments:

"The reliance on authority is a universal German quality. It can't just be a question of mentality, it must also come from education. . . . Perhaps because our democratic institutions are not old enough, because participation in government power and positive criticism on the part of the opposition are things people just have to get used to. . . . At first we had a dictatorship and now we have a democracy. If it is to endure we must make an effort to turn it into a real component of our thinking. Take a look at the NPD, I mean, the susceptibility of the Germans to extremist ideas without rational content. A little group of that kind can always create a stir and unfortunately the bulk of our people give them too little thought. This awful political apathy. The people just say to themselves: We voted for Adenauer, then we voted for Erhard, and then we voted for Kiesinger, so they would attend to politics for us. That's what I mean by reliance on authority. There's too little commitment." (pp.132-3)

Fortunately so far the economic conditions which would favour the growth of the 'little group', unlike Hitler's little group in the late 1920s, do not exist. Moreover Dr Werner Paulsen, aged thirty-two and a member of the FDP (Freie Deutsche Partei) warns against the dangers of consensus politics:

"The alliance between the SPD and the CDU (1966) for example: the Great Coalition. This strikes us as dangerous from a democratic point of view. . . . The NPD is not a union of the former small right-wing groups and parties, it is composed of the DRP (Deutsch Reichspartei), the Gesamtdeutsche Partei, the FDP and the BHE (Band der Heimatvertriebenenen and Entrechtete) and many individuals who have never belonged to any party. Both in Germany and abroad the NPD is accused of being a Nazi party. This is not true." (p.139)

Yet, as Nora Beloff remarked in the *Observer* of 2 April 1972 about the importance of Brandt's Ostpolitik succeeding if extremist solutions are not once again to threaten Germany: "We cannot yet afford to take the new Germany's conversion to our democratic values for granted. We cannot assume that when the children of those who went to Hitler's schools turn to violence, they are just soft-headed liberals like so many student-rebels nearer home."

As this psycho-history of Germany draws to a close, it would seem appropriate to glance at the education of "the children of those who went to Hitler's schools"; the former were primary and secondary school pupils between 1946 and 1956 and are now adult German citizens aged between twenty-five and thirty-five, but we must also take into consideration the generation succeeding theirs, spread over the last sixteen years. Only a minority of the parents of the first group and none of those who are parents of the second group would have been old enough to have fought in the Second World War. Yet they and their children inherited the direct legacies of Germany's participation in that war. Children growing up in either of the two Germanies in the 1950s and 1960s must therefore be thought of as the products of homes and schools thus conditioned, with all that this can imply for the patterns of their educational development. This again needs to be viewed in the perspective of the psycho-historical tradition of German society already sketched. "If you are separated from your opposites," wrote the poet Yeats in 'A Vision', "you consume yourself away." That, it has been suggested, has been the malady, 'separation from her opposites', which has coloured Germany's political, economic and cultural story.

Let us take a look at how this tendency had manifested itself on the German educational scene. The main features can be swiftly summarised: at the level of the primary school teacher the tradition of the skilled craftsman rather than the independent practitioner, at the secondary level the over-weening influence of Prussia and the academic Gymnasium-Wielwisserei being the perverted form of Allgemeine Bildung, in teacher training the denominational split between Roman Catholic and Protestant and recently Communist and non-Communist, at university level the glory of Akademische Freiheit, the efficiency of the Technische Hochschule and the arrogant tyranny of the Herr Professor, in the field of vocational education the splendid legacy of Kerschensteiner. With regard to the immediate past and the present one basic factor must be stressed, namely that although the pedagogical terminology is similar, the pedagogical principles and practices of the German Federal Republic and the German Democratic Republic are diametrically opposed to each other. Quite simply spelt out, this means that children have been growing up for the last two decades with two completely different *Weltanschauungen* according to where they have been domiciled: in the East a Communist, secular, totalitarian version of man's role in the universe, in the West a liberal-social-democratic, semi-humanist and Christian, pluralistic version. Both systems may be criticised for different reasons, the former for lack of charity, the latter for lack of integrated purpose.

An article in the *Times* of 29 January 1972 had an illuminating comment on an OECD report on education in the GFR, which it found 'under-financed and élitist':

"The team were especially worried that the right-wing dogmatism of the older generation of teachers was now being replaced by an equally dangerous left-wing dogmatism among the younger teachers. [author's comment: another separation of opposites] It is certainly true that the deficiences and social injustices of the system, the failure to provide a convincing education in liberal democracy, and the somewhat blind anti-communism of some older teachers, are driving more and more young teachers to the left. This trend is encouraged by the example of East Germany, where the educational system was completely reorganised after the war, with a new generation of teachers. In spite of its ideological content it had features which highlight West German deficiencies. West Germany should not be afraid to learn a few things from its communist rival if they help to strengthen the foundations of the democratic system by producing a better educated citizenry."

Across the vast span of some two thousand years, of which we have been making a study in miniature, what are the constants and variables in the psycho-historical constitution of that German citizenry?

With the needle of psychological analysis I have been probing the nature of early German history and modern German history with special reference to the Hitler phenomenon: its sources, manifestations and consequences. I have been looking for and finding at least some traces of a significant correspondence between the unconscious or semi-conscious functioning of recent and contemporary Germans and their historical past. There has been evidence of the existence of that 'transpersonal dimension of consciousness', mentioned by Rollo May, the negative aspect being one of regression as exemplified in the barbarism of the Thirty Years' War and the Nazi concentration camps, the positive aspect being one of illumination as exemplified in the music of Bach or the poetry of Rilke.

"The real continuity of history (see p.84) in its German context has been illustrated by pointing to the reappearance of similar archetypal figures, parental, heroic, evil, sexual and mystical: Mother Courage, Barbarossa, Hindenburg; Siegfried, Frederick the Great, Goethe, Helmust von Moltke; Kriemhild, Brunhilde, Tristan, Isolde; Hagen, Hitler, the Puer Aeternus in the Wandervogel.

Burckhardt's general thesis about "the life and death of societies" being determined by the "dynamics of man's life" seems to have received ample confirmation in the evidence provided by the life and death of the Weimar Republic. This is also true of Jung's "cultural context determining the structure of human personality": because of the role of the army and the prevalence of the military code within the German state, children in home and school were pressed into behaving in a *'stramm'* (rigidly tough) fashion: the personality structures of the characters in Christopher Isherwood's *Good-bye to Berlin*, as he so deftly shows, were determined by the cultural context of that city in the late 1920s and early 1930s.

Reverting in conclusion to Schrödinger's point (p.85) that "you in a sense were the whole", we may reflect on the affinities not only between German characters of different historical epochs, but also between them and the psycho-historian who is the author of this book. Love between humans as symbolised by Gottfried of Strasbourg in the twelfth century (Tristan and Isolde), Goethe in the eighteenth century (Faust and Gretchen) and Musil in the twentieth century (Ulrich and Agathe) and love as experienced by us moderns are not mere parts of the same whole, but they are the whole in the sense of the kind of historical interpretation here employed. All historical and personal variables, whether in Strasbourg, Weimar or Vienna, are informed by archetypal constants: the psycho-historian's success may be measured by the degree to which he makes a union between the subject he studies, in this case German history, and his own personality and the personalities of his readers. Does this conclusion in fact mean that the knowledge I have gained of myself and the knowledge I have gained from my study of German history have fused and become one? Do I understand better where I belong in history, what history is all about and how there is an ultimate purpose in human existence? I suppose that unless I believed that this book provided affirmative answers to these questions, I would not have presumed to write it.

Chapter Notes

FOREWORD

1 R. S. Thomas: *Poetry for Supper* (Hart Davis, London 1964)

CHAPTER ONE

1 Freya Stark: 'Lunch with Homer' *Encounter* (March 1968)
2 C. G. Jung: *Memories, Dreams and Reflections,* page 18 (Collins and Routledge & Kegan Paul, London 1963)
3 Monica Blackett: *The Mark of the Maker: A Portrait of Helen Waddell,* Appendix I (Constable, London 1973)
4 Hermann Broch: *The Sleepwalkers,* page 80 (Martin & Secker, London 1932)
5 C. G. Jung: *Contributions to Analytical Psychology,* tr. by H. G. Cary, page 118-119 (F. Baynes, London 1928, 1942, 1945)
6 C. G. Jung: *Collected Works,* Vol. 5, Symbols of Transformation — an Analysis of the Prelude to a case of Schizophrenia, tr. by R. F. C. Hill, page xxiv (Routledge & Kegan Paul, London 1956)
7 Rainer Maria Rilke: *Letters,* tr. by Green & Norton, Vol. II, page 342, (New York 1945)
8 C. G. Jung: *Contributions to Analytical Psychology,* tr. by H. G. Cary, page 365 (F. Baynes, London 1928, 1942, 1945)
9 *Ibid.,* page 246
10 I am indebted to G. Adler for the phrases 'conscious' and 'unconscious anominity'. See G. Adler: *Studies in Analytical Psychology,* page 127 (Routledge & Kegan Paul, London 1948)
11 R. C. Johnson: *The Imprisoned Splendour: An Approach to Reality* (Hodder & Stoughton, London 1953)
12 I. Progoff: *Jung's Psychology and its Social Meaning,* page 232 (Routledge & Kegan Paul, London 1953)
13 N. Berdyaev: *The Meaning of History,* page 17 (Bles, London 1936)
14 William Rose: *Rainer Rilke: Aspects of his Mind and Poetry* (London 1939)

15 *Selected Letters of Rainer Maria Rilke 1902-1926,* tr. by R. F. C. Hull, page 264-5 (London 1946)
16 Eliade: *Cosmos and History, the Myth of the Eternal Return* (Harper Torch Books, New York 1959)

CHAPTER TWO

1 Rilke: *Third Duino Elegy*
2 J. Campbell: *The Masks of God,* Vol. I, page 12 (Secker & Warburg, London 1960)
3 Teilhard de Chardin: *The Phenomenon of Man,* page 221 (Collins, London 1959)
4 J. Huxley: *The Two Cultures,* a letter to *Encounter* (June 1960)
5 Ian Suttie: *The Origins of Love and Hate* (Pelican Books, London 1960)
6 J. Campbell: *op. cit.* pages 117-118
7 Max Plowman: *Bridge Into the Future,* page 135 (Dakers, London 1944)
8 R. G. Collingwood: *The Idea of History* (Oxford University Press, Oxford 1946)
9 Thomas Blackburn: *The Next Word* (London 1958)
10 Eliade: *Cosmos and History, the Myth of the Eternal Return,* pages 44-46 (Harper Torch Books, New York 1959)
11 Hugh Lawrence: *Tales of an Old Yew Tree* (Stories Old and New, Blackie and Son Ltd., New York 1909)
12 C. G. Jung: *Collected Works,* Vol. 5, *Symbols of Transformation,* pages 389-90 (Routledge & Kegan Paul, London 1956)
13 C. G. Jung: *Collected Works,* Vol. 17, *The Development of the Personality,* page 45 (Routledge & Kegan Paul, London 1954)
14 Erich Neumann: *The Origins and History of Consciousness,* page xxii ff. (Routledge & Kegan Paul, London 1954)

CHAPTER THREE

1 Erik H. Erikson: *Identity. Youth and Crisis* (Faber & Faber, London 1968)
2 Erich Neumann: *The Origins of History and Consciousness,* page 131 (Routledge & Kegan Paul, London 1954)
3 J. Hawkes: *The Crystalline Society,* an article in *New Statesman and Nation* (25 September 1948)
4 H. G. Baynes: *The Mythology of the Soul,* page 425 (Methuen, London 1949)
5 H. G. Baynes: *op. cit.,* pages 398-9
6 Longfellow: *Hiawatha*

7   C. G. Jung: *Collected Works*, Vol. 5 *Symbols of Transformation*, page 357 (Routledge & Kegan Paul, London 1956)

8   C. G. Jung: *Flying Saucers: A Modern Myth of Things Seen in the Sky*, tr. by R. F. L. Hull, page 85 (Routledge & Kegan Paul, London 1959)

9   W. B. Stanford: *The Ulysses Theme: a Study in the Adapatability of a Traditional Hero* (Blackwell, Oxford 1954)

10 Nikos Kazantzakis: *The Odyssey — a Modern Sequel*, tr. by Kimin Friar (Secker & Warburg, 1958)

11 T. S. Eliot: *The Waste Land* (Probsthain, London 1965)

12 P. W. Martin: *Experiment in Depth*, pages 76-7 (Routledge & Kegan Paul, London 1955)

13 Simone Weil: *Notebooks*, Vol. II, page 414 (London 1956)

14 Rainer Maria Rilke: *The Eighth Duino Elegy*, tr. by J. B. Leishman and S. Spender, pages 33-4 (Hogarth Press, London 1957)

15 Denis de Rougemont: *The Devil's Share* (Pantheon Books, New York 1944)

16 From a report on one of Jung's Zurich seminars

17 From a report on one of Jung's Zurich seminars

18 Eric Neumann: *The Origins and History of Consciousness*, page 221 (Routledge & Kegan Paul, London 1954)

19 *Ibid.*, page 295

20 J. Campbell: *The Hero with a Thousand Faces* (Pantheon Books, New York 1949)

21 J. Middleton Murray: *Heaven and Earth*, page 147 (Cape, London 1938)

22 N. Krupskaya: *Memories of Lenin*, tr. by E. Verney (Lawrence & Wishart, London 1970)

23 Erik Erikson: *Gandhi's Truth* (Faber & Faber, London 1970)

24 Alan Bullock: *Hitler: A Study in Tyranny*, Epilogue, page 735 (Odhams Press, London 1952)

25 Dr. H. Zimmer: *Integrating the Evil*, Lecture No. 39, Guild of Pastoral Psychology, London

26 G. Marcel: *Men Against Humanity*, page 27 (Harvill Press, London 1953)

27 Wordsworth: *The Prelude*, Book V

28 Lewis Mumford: *The Condition of Man*, page 276 (Secker & Warburg, London 1944)

29 Gai Eaton: *The Richest Vein* (Faber & Faber, London 1949)

30 Laurens Van der Post: *The Dark Eye in Africa*, page 92 (Hogarth Press, London 1955)

CHAPTER FOUR

1   Carolyn G. Heilbrun: *Towards Androgyny, Aspects of Male and Female in Literature* (Gollanz, London 1973)

2 Arianna Stassinopoulos: *The Female Woman* (Davis Poynter, London 1973)

3 Homer: *Iliad* III, tr. by E. V. Rieu, page 68 (Penguin Classics, London 1955)

4 Helcn Waddell: *Peter Abelard*, page 25 (Constable, London, 1925)

5 Etienne Gilson: *Heloise and Abelard*, tr. by K. L. Shook, page 47 (Hollis & Carter, London 1953)

6 G. Thibon: *Le qui Dieu a Uni*, page 129 (Claudendot, Paris 1947)

CHAPTER FIVE

1 W. Herberg: 'God and the Theologians' *Encounter* (November 1963)

2 Erich Heller: *The Ironic German*, page 25 (Secker & Warburg, London 1958)

3 Philip Leon: *Beyond Belief and Unbelief: Creative Nihilism* (Gollancz, London 1965)

4 Hendrick Kraemer: *World Cultures and World Religions*, page 159 (Lutterworth Press, London 1960)

5 Sir Herbert Read: *Icon and Idea* (Faber, London 1955)

6 *Icon and Idea*, pages 91-3

7 *Op. cit.*, page 106

8 *Op. cit.*, page 138

9 *Op. cit.*, page 124

10 Erich Neumann: *Art and the Creative Unconscious*, page 133 (Routledge & Kegan Paul, London 1959)

11 Margaret Masterman: *Theism as a Scientific Hypothesis*, in *Theoria to Theory*, Vol. I, (Epiphany Philosophers, Cambridge 1966)

12 Suzuki: *Mysticism, Christian and Buddhist*, page 147 (Allen & Unwin, London 1957)

13 C. G. Jung: *The Structure and Dynamics of the Psyche*, Collected Works Vol. 8, pages 223-5; Vol. 9 Part II, Chapter IV "The Self", (Routledge & Kegan Paul, London)

14 Lewis Mumford: *The Human Prospect*, pages 40-1 (Secker & Warburg, London 1956)

15 Maud Bodkin: *Studies of Type-Images in Poetry, Religion and Philosophy* (Oxford University Press, London 1951)

16 Max Plowman: *The Right to Live, What Death Means to Me* (Andrew Daker, 1947)

17 Max Knoll: *Transformation of Science in Our Age*. Eranos Yearbook No. 3, *Man and Time* (Routledge & Kegan Paul, London 1956)

18 Sir Alister Hardy: *The Living Stream: A Restatement of Evolutionary Theory and its Relations to the Spirit of Man* (Collins, London 1965)

19 *Op. cit.,* page 21
20 *Hibbert Journal* Vol. 47, pages 10-13 (Allen & Unwin, London 1949)
21 Hardy, *op. cit.,* page 282
22 *Op. cit.,* page 284
23 *Op. cit.,* page 283

CHAPTER SIX

1 Vol. III, page 227 (Kegan Paul, French Trubner and Co., London 1819)
 2 George Steiner: *In Bluebeard's Castle* (Faber, London 1971)
 3 E. Neumann: *The Origins and History of Consciousness* (Routledge & Kegan Paul, 1954); Gerhard Adler: *Studies in Analytical Psychology* (Routledge & Kegan Paul, 1948); and Robert S. McCully *Research Theory and Symbolism* (Williams & Wilkins, Baltimore, 1971)
 4 Rollo May: *Love and Will* (Norton and Co., New York, 1970)
 5 Mircea Eliade: *Cosmos and History: The Myth of the Eternal Return* (Harper Torch Books, New York 1970)
 6 I. Progoff: *Jung's Psychology and its Social Meaning* (Routledge & Kegan Paul, 1953)
 7 Burckhardt: *Forces and Freedom: An Interpretation of History* (Meridan Books, New York 1955)
 8 Jung: *Civilisation in Transition: Collected Works;* Vol. XX (Routledge & Kegan Paul, London 1959)
 9 Erwin Schrödinger: *My View of the World* (Cambridge University Press, London 1964)
10 Frank Field: *The Last Days of Mankind. Karl Kraus and his Vienna* (Macmillan, London 1967)
11 Professor Scarisbrick (Pelican Biographies, London 1971)
12 Flugel: *Psychoanalysis and History,* page 124 ff (Prentice Hall, Englewood Cliffs, N.J. 1963)
13 Norman Brown: *Life Against Death, the Psycho-analytical Meaning of History* (Routledge & Kegan Paul, London 1959)
14 Robert Jay Lifton: *Thought Reform and the Psychology of Totalism: A Study of Brainwashing in China and Revolutionary Immortality* (Weidenfeld & Nicolson, London 1968)
15 Erik Erikson: *Childhood and Society* (Pelican Books, London 1970)
16 Erik Erikson: *Gandhi's Truth* (Faber, London 1970)
17 Jack Kovel: *White Racism, a Psycho-History* (Allen Lane, The Penguin Press, London 1970)
18 Lucille Iremonger: *The Fiery Chariot: a Study of British Prime Ministers and the Search for Love* (Secker & Warburg, London 1970)

19 *Education for World Understanding, an Appendix on Thomas More and Thomas Cromwell* (Pergamon Press, Oxford 1968)

CHAPTER SEVEN

1 E. M. Forster: *Aspects of the Novel* (Arnold, London 1949)
2 *Daily Telegraph* review (1961)
3 Karl Kraus: *The Book of Austria*, page 405 (Osterreuchische Staatsdruckerei, Vienna 1958)
4 Robert Musil: *The Man Without Qualities,* Vols. I, II, III, tr. by Eithne Wilkins and Ernst Kaiser (Secker & Warburg, London 1961, 1965)
5 English translation by Wilkins and Kaiser, Vol. I, page 64 (Secker & Warburg, London)
6 Heimito von Döderer: *The Demons* Vols. I, II, tr. by Richard and Clare Winston (Knopf, New York 1961)
7 Rose Macaulay: *They were Defeated* (Collins, London 1960)
8 The Shorter Novels of Herman Melville: *Benito Cereno* (Grosset's Universal Library, New York 1928)

CHAPTER EIGHT

1 Ogg: *The Reformation,* page 30 (Benn, London 1930)
2 *Ibid.,* page 33
3 M. Balfour: *The Kaiser and his Times,* page 26 (Cresset Press, London 1964)
4 Ritter: *Staatskunst und Kriegshandwerk* (Munich 1954-8)
5 J. Campbell: *The Masks of God,* Vol. IV, page 5 (Secker & Warburg, London 1968)
6 For this and other quoted passages, see Gottfried von Strasbourg: *Tristan with the 'Tristan' of Thomas,* tr. by A. T. Haltu (Penguin Classics, London 1960)
7 *The Masks of God* Vol. IV, pages 67 ff
8 Erik H. Erikson: *Young Man Luther — A Study in Psycho-Analytic History* (Faber, London 1959)
9 Erich Heller: Essay on 'Goethe and the Avoidance of Tragedy' from *The Disinherited Mind* (Bowes and Bowes, Cambridge 1952)
10 Thomas Mann: *Last Essays;* page 124 (Knopf, New York 1959)
11 Heller, *op. cit.*
12 Barraclough: *The Origins of Modern Germany,* page 412 (Blackwell, London 1947)
13 Bertrand Russell: *Freedom and Organisation,* pages 389-505 (Allen & Unwin, London 1934)
14 Baraclough, *ibid.,* page 443
15 E. von Eyck: *The Weimar Republic,* Vol. 1, page 343 (Harvard University Press, 1962)

16 Howard Becker: *German Youth, Bond or Free* (Kegan Paul, London 1949)

17 Heller *op. cit.*, page 29

18 Heller *op. cit.*, page 105

19 Heller *op. cit.*, page 140

20 Odon von Horvath: *A Child of Our Times* (Methuen, London 1938)

21 For this and subsequent quotations, see *The Letters of Thomas Mann* (Secker & Warburg, London 1973)

22 Heller: *Mann, The Ironic German* (Secker & Warburg, London 1958)

23 Thomas Mann: *The Magic Mountain*, (Penguin Modern Classics, London 1971)

24 K. D. Bracher: *The German Dictatorship: The Origins, Structure and Consequences of National Socialism* (Weidenfeld & Nicolson, London 1969)

25 Bracher, *ibid.*, page 191

26 James Douglas-Hamilton: *Motive for a Mission, the Story Behind Hess's Flight to Britain* (Macmillan, London 1971)

27 *Inside the Third Reich*, tr. by R. & C. Winston page 570 (Weidenfeld & Nicolson, London 1970)

28 Steiner: *In Bluebeard's Castle*, page 31 (Faber, London 1971)

29 *Op. cit.*, page 247

30 Bernard Levin: *The Times*, 14 December, 1971

31 Robert Donington: *Wagner's Ring and Its Symbols, the Music and the Myth* (Faber, London 1963)

32 Erik H. Erikson: *Childhood and Society* (Pelican Books, London 1970)

33 Ernst Toller: *Letters from Prison* (London, 1936)

34 Alfred Weber: *Farewell to European History* (Routledge & Kegan Paul, London 1947)

35 C. G. Jung: *Collected Works*, Vol. X Chap. III "Civilisation in Transition" (Routledge & Kegan Paul, London 1972)

36 Bertholt Brecht: *Selected Poems.* Translation and introduction by H. R. Hays (Evergreen Books, London 1960)

37 Thomas Mann: *Dr Faustus*, pages 480-2 (Secker & Warburg, London 1949)

38 Most of the material in this section is reworked from a doctoral thesis presented at London University in 1955 and entitled: "The Career of Adolf Reichwein — A Study of Socio-Political Tensions in German Education Between 1918 and 1945."

39 Christopher Sykes: *Troubled Loyalty: A Biography of Adam von Trott* (Collins, London 1968)

40 Christabel Bielenberg: *The Past is Myself* (Chatto, London 1968)

41 J. Wheeler Bennett: *The Nemesis of Power* (Macmillan, London 1964)
42 Günther Grass: *The Tin Drum* (1959, Secker & Warburg, London 1962)
43 See the GER VALE Lecture by the author, 1958, GER Archives, London University Institute of Education
44 Siegfried Lenz: *The German Lesson* (Macdonald, London 1971)
45 Michael Balfour: *West Germany* (Benn, London 1968)
46 Jurgen Nevu-du-Mont: *After Hitler: Report from a West German City* (Allen Lane, London 1968)

Bibliography

Barraclough, G., An Introduction to Contemporary History (*Watts, London 1964*)

Brown, Norman O., Life Against Death. The Psycho-Analytical Meaning of History (*Routledge & Kegan Paul, London 1959*)

Campbell, Joseph, The Masks of God (*4 Volumes—Secker & Warburg, London 1968*); Myths to Live by (*Souvenir Press, London 1972*)

Donington, R., Wagner's Ring and its Symbols. The Music and the Myth (*Faber, London 1963*)

Eliade, M., Cosmos and History. The Myth of the Eternal Return (*Harper Torch Books, Harper, New York 1959*)

Erikson, Erik, Childhood and Society (*Pelican Books, London 1970*)

Heilbrun, C. G., Towards Androgyny-Aspects of Male and Female in Literature (*Gollancz, London 1973*)

Heller, E., The Disinherited Mind (*Bowes and Bowes, Cambridge 1952*)

Kovel, J., White Racism. A Psycho-History (*Allen Lane, London 1970*)

Lenz, S., The German Lesson (Novel) (*Macdonald, London 1971*)

Marcel, G., Men Against Humanity (*The Harvill Press, London 1952*)

McGlashan, Alan, The Savage and Beautiful Country (*Chatto & Windus, London 1966*)

Mumford, Lewis, The Myth of the Machine-Technics and Human Development (*Secker and Warburg, London 1967*)

Neumann, E., The Origins and History of Consciousness (*Routledge & Kegan Paul, London 1954*)

Plumb, J. H., The Death of the Past (*Macmillan, London 1969*)

Poulet, G., Studies in Human Time (*John Hopkins Press, Baltimore 1956*)

Read, Herbert, Icon and Idea. The Function of Art in the Development of Human Consciousness (*Faber, London 1955*)

Roszak, T., Where the Wasteland Ends: Politics and Transcendence in Post-Industrial Society. (*Faber, London 1973*)

Stanford, W. B., The Ulysses Theme. A Study in the Adaptability of a Traditional Hero (*Blackwell, Oxford 1954*)

Steiner, George, In Bluebeard's Castle (*Faber, London 1971*)

Weil, Simone, Selected Essays 1934-43 (*Oxford University Press, London 1962*)